WHAT YOUR COLLEAGUES ARE SAYING . . .

"The power of intriguing texts, purposeful reading, and development of independence in reading are the keystones of this book. Teachers will find guidance on how to snag the interest of middle school students with content texts especially written by David Harrison and woven into compelling lessons by Laura Robb. The authors provide teachers with a powerhouse of lessons that nudge students along in becoming independent readers who can infer, summarize, discern cause and effect, and much more. Not only will students gain skill in reading, but they will also have multiple opportunities to write, discuss, and broaden their vocabulary. An outstanding resource!"

—**Mary Jo Fresch**, PhD, professor emeritus at the College of Education and Human Ecology, The Ohio State University

"This book shows teachers how to apprentice developing readers into knowing and doing the secret things that expert readers know and do. Laura Robb and David L. Harrison have nailed the very core of the kind of cognitive apprenticeship that transforms student engagement and capacity: provide guided practice into the use of new stances and strategies (in ways tailored to meet the needs of the whole class, small groups, and individuals), and then move to deliberate independent practice that consolidates, extends, and explores these moves of expert readers."

—**Jeffrey Wilhelm**, author of *Planning Powerful Instruction* and *Diving Deep Into Nonfiction*

"With special consideration on our students who are developing as proficient readers, this book unpacks an essential step in skilled teaching—the guided practice component. So often, we leapfrog from modeling to independent practice; Laura Robb and David L. Harrison's thoughtful inquiry into guided practice helps us understand the power and promise of guided practice, the essential components of guided practice, and model lessons to enact guided practice."

—**Molly Ness**, PhD, author of *Think Big With Think Alouds* and *Every Minute Matters*

"Laura Robb and David Harrison's new book is a great practical guide to help teachers provide more effective reading instruction!"

—**Larry Ferlazzo**, high school teacher, author, and *Education Week* columnist

"In *Guided Practice for Reading Growth* teacher expertise is valued, empathy for developing readers is in the forefront, and a system for guided practice comes to life with lessons and examples to try right away. Laura Robb and David L. Harrison have brought us a professional resource to help with the important steps between modeling and independent practice so that all students can experience growth and confidence."

—**Gravity Goldberg**, author of *Teach Like Yourself* and *What Do I Teach Readers Tomorrow?*

"I loved teaching the guided practice lessons because it was easy to make them work for my students. Teachers with little experience and teachers like me, with thirty years experience, will find the lessons easy to present because each one is organized with clear directions and choices. My students loved learning about poetic devices, different kinds of poetry, and they understood figurative language because David Harrison is a master at weaving it into his poems. I loved having the purpose up front as it clarified my thinking. All of my students thoroughly enjoyed building their background knowledge with the recommended videos—this is such a great idea for developing readers!"

—**Stacey Yost**, fifth grade inclusion teacher, Winchester, VA

T0354086

"The lessons included everything I needed to improve students' reading and vocabulary and to engage them in thinking about the poems and short texts. All my students were motivated to read the texts, especially after watching the video. The skills aligned with our state standards, and students learned so much about figurative language and different kinds of poems. I loved that the questions students discussed were always high level and nudged students to think deeply. The repeated readings woven into the lessons were a boost to students' fluency. Spacing the lessons over three days allowed students to absorb information and increased their motivation to complete them."

—**Bridget Wilson**, fifth-grade inclusion teacher in Winchester, VA

"My ESOL students appreciated the *cold writing* I did in my notebook because it gave them a model to study, discuss, and learn from. I loved that Laura Robb encourages teachers to have students draw to show their understanding of vocabulary and interpretive questions. The writing supports the visualizing students do while reading, and they loved the active learning—the students did the work and they improved with citing text evidence to support a position, enlarged their vocabulary, and were able to self-evaluate to show how and why their reading improved. The more they wrote and discussed, the greater their insights and critical thinking."

—**Wanda Waters**, ESOL teacher in Winchester, VA

GUIDED PRACTICE FOR
READING GROWTH

GRADES 4-8

For my granddaughter, Helena,
with love and thanks for all she has taught me about developing readers.—LR

To struggling readers, on the day they hold the first book they ever read by
themselves, and can say, "I did it!"—DLH

GUIDED PRACTICE FOR
READING GROWTH

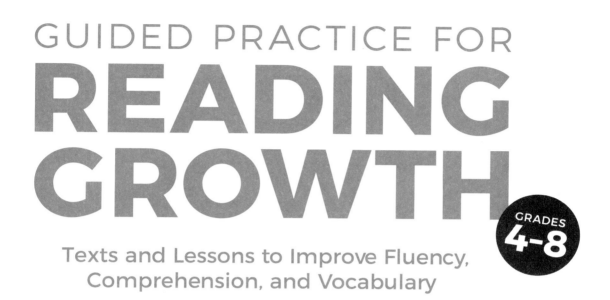

GRADES
4-8

Texts and Lessons to Improve Fluency, Comprehension, and Vocabulary

LAURA ROBB · DAVID L. HARRISON

Foreword by Timothy Rasinski

resources.corwin.com/guidedpractice

CORWIN Literacy

FOR INFORMATION:

Corwin

A SAGE Company

2455 Teller Road

Thousand Oaks, California 91320

(800) 233-9936

www.corwin.com

SAGE Publications Ltd.

1 Oliver's Yard

55 City Road

London EC1Y 1SP

United Kingdom

SAGE Publications India Pvt. Ltd.

B 1/I 1 Mohan Cooperative Industrial Area

Mathura Road, New Delhi 110 044

India

SAGE Publications Asia-Pacific Pte. Ltd.

18 Cross Street #10-10/11/12

China Square Central

Singapore 048423

Printed in the United States of America

ISBN 978-1-5443-9849-5

Director and Publisher, Corwin Classroom: Lisa Luedeke

Senior Acquisitions Editor: Tori Bachman

Editorial Development Manager: Julie Nemer

Associate Content Development Editor: Sharon Wu

Production Editor: Amy Schroller

Copy Editor: Ashley E. Horne

Typesetter: C&M Digitals (P) Ltd.

Proofreader: Dennis Webb

Indexer: Integra

Cover Designer: Scott Van Atta

Marketing Manager: Deena Meyer

This book is printed on acid-free paper.

SUSTAINABLE FORESTRY INITIATIVE
Certified Chain of Custody
Promoting Sustainable Forestry
www.sfiprogram.org
SFI-01268

20 21 22 23 24 10 9 8 7 6 5 4 3 2 1

CONTENTS

PART III NEXT STEPS FOR GUIDED PRACTICE AND GROWTH IN READING

Visit the companion website at
resources.corwin.com/guidedpractice
for downloadable resources and videos.

LIST OF VIDEOS

Note From the Publisher: The authors have provided video and web content throughout the book that is available to you through QR (quick response) codes. To read a QR code, you must have a smartphone or tablet with a camera. We recommend that you download a QR code reader app that is made specifically for your phone or tablet brand.

Videos may also be accessed at **resources.corwin.com/guidedpractice**

Lesson Number	Lesson Title	Video Title	Video URL
1	Partner Discussion Using the Poem for Two Voices, "What Was She Thinking?"	First Look at Jane	https://youtu.be/rcL4jnGTL1U
3	Partner Discussions Using the Poem, "Escape Artist"	Houdini Rope Escape	https://youtu.be/EbvZZsYZmEY
3	Partner Discussions Using the Poem, "Escape Artist"	Harry Houdini—Straight Jacket Escape	https://youtu.be/3r8qr-p9z5g
3	Partner Discussions Using the Poem, "Escape Artist"	Circus Stardust Entertainment Agency Presents: Flying Trapeze	https://youtu.be/Gi9ky8CBBzc
4	Partner Discussions Using the Text, "What Was Early Humans' Greatest Invention?"	Early Man and His Life	https://youtu.be/1S9XZGlupvw
5	Partner Discussions Using the Poem, "Before I Could Write This Poem—"	The Beginning of Everything—The Big Bang	https://youtu.be/wNDGgL73ihY
5	Partner Discussions Using the Poem, "Before I Could Write This Poem—"	Tsunamis 101	https://youtu.be/_oPb_9gOdn4
7	Partner Discussions of the Poem, "The Explorers"	Age of Exploration	https://youtu.be/17OP-2eSW5M
8	Partner Discussions of the Short Text, "The Day I Started Becoming an American"	Ellis Island	https://youtu.be/hlHGDw14JZ8

Lesson Number	Lesson Title	Video Title	Video URL
8	Partner Discussions of the Short Text, "The Day I Started Becoming an American"	"Tour of a Lifetime" of Statue of Liberty	https://youtu.be/F3wjRQDQnzk
9	Partner Discussions of the Poem, "Ode to the Skunk"	Smelly Truth About Skunks	https://youtu.be/wNGMyaxPltc
10	Partner Discussions for the Text, "I Am Not a Number"	Positively Homeless Family Homelessness in America	https://youtu.be/j32IEpYvqvA
11	Partner Discussions of the Short Text, "Now . . . and Then"	One-Room Schoolhouses in America	https://youtu.be/AoieZKCVm-w
12	Partner Discussions Using the Poem, "If Stones Had Tongues"	The History of Stonehenge for Kids: Stonehenge for Children	https://youtu.be/wf7xwHFuH2o
13	Shared Reading of the Poem, "The Man for the Job"	George Washington—First U.S. President	https://youtu.be/hvE9fb--Dig
14	Shared Reading of the Short Text, "Jane Goodall: A Portrait of Determination"	Jane Goodall Tribute	https://youtu.be/06M7hggEz7k
15	Shared Reading of the Poem, "Rain, She"	Rain Forests 101	https://youtu.be/3vijLre760w
16	Shared Reading of the Short Text, "The Service Dog: Man's Best Friend"	The Puppies Go To The Farm	https://youtu.be/mW1-SbxTQiU
17	Shared Reading of the Poem, "Lost and Found"	Opera Singer Defies Odds to Become Promising Star	https://youtu.be/gNeed2jo3No
18	Shared Reading of the Short Text, "Johnny Appleseed—Jonathan Chapman: One Man—Two Stories"	Johnny Appleseed	https://youtu.be/bg6wXWOlNyc
19	Shared Reading of the Poem, "George Washington Carver"	George Washington Carver "The Plant Doctor" Revolutionized Farming Industry	https://youtu.be/sdz8XTNttdc
20	Shared Reading of the Short Text, "The Masters of Pollination"	Bee Pollination—A Beautiful Natural Act	https://youtu.be/9Zbq3KB4Mpl

(Continued)

(Continued)

Lesson Number	Lesson Title	Video Title	Video URL
21	Shared Reading of the Poem, "Amazon Rain Forest"	Amazon River	https://youtu.be/zSfDksLJ7I4
22	Shared Reading of the Short Text, "Chita Rivera: The Dancer's Dancer"	Chita Rivera Performs "America" and "All That Jazz"	https://youtu.be/e2E30HG5QNs
22	Shared Reading of the Short Text, "Chita Rivera: The Dancer's Dancer"	Broadway 101: What Is a Broadway Theatre?	https://youtu.be/9jNOwh8Qgt4
23	Shared Reading of the Poem, "Who Were They—Those First People to Walk Upon This Land?"	Peopling the Americas	https://youtu.be/jaizoayO9yU
24	Shared Reading of the Short Text, "Solving an Ancient Cave Mystery"	What Is an Ice Age?	https://youtu.be/dJ5GYQrkvxI
24	Shared Reading of the Short Text, "Solving an Ancient Cave Mystery"	Ice Age Cave	https://youtu.be/J50KJ7304ps

SKILL LESSON CHART

Skill	Lesson Title	Page Number
Analyzing narrative	Lesson 6: Partner Discussions of the Short Narrative, "Manhunt"	57
	Lesson 17: Shared Reading of the Poem, "Lost and Found"	93
Comparing/ contrasting	Lesson 11: Partner Discussions of the Short Text, "Now . . . and Then"	72
	Lesson 18: Shared Reading of the Short Text, "Johnny Appleseed—Jonathan Chapman: One Man—Two Stories"	97
	Lesson 24: Shared Reading the Short Text, "Solving an Ancient Cave Mystery"	115
Determining cause/effect	Lesson 17: Shared Reading of the Poem, "Lost and Found"	93
Determining important information/ recalling details	Lesson 1: Partner Discussions Using the Poem for Two Voices, "What Was She Thinking?"	40
	Lesson 4: Partner Discussions Using the Text, "What Was Early Humans' Greatest Invention?"	51
	Lesson 7: Partner Discussions of the Poem, "The Explorers"	60
	Lesson 13: Shared Reading of the Poem, "The Man for the Job"	80
	Lesson 14: Shared Reading of the Short Text, "Jane Goodall: A Portrait of Determination"	83
	Lesson 19: Shared Reading of the Poem, "George Washington Carver"	100
	Lesson 20: Shared Reading of the Short Text, "The Masters of Pollination"	103
	Lesson 22: Shared Reading of the Short Text, "Chita Rivera: The Dancer's Dancer"	109
Determining main ideas	Lesson 5: Partner Discussions Using the Poem, "Before I Could Write This Poem—"	54
	Lesson 12: Partner Discussions Using the Poem, "If Stones Had Tongues"	76
	Lesson 21: Shared Reading of the Poem, "Amazon Rain Forest"	106
	Lesson 23: Shared Reading of the Poem, "Who Were They—Those First People to Walk Upon This Land?"	112
	Lesson 24: Shared Reading of the Short Text, "Solving an Ancient Cave Mystery"	115

(Continued)

(Continued)

Skill	Lesson Title	Page Number
Determining problem/ solution	Lesson 20: Shared Reading of the Short Text, "The Masters of Pollination"	103
Developing vocabulary and word building	All Lessons	
Discussing open-ended questions	Lesson 7: Partner Discussions of the Poem, "The Explorers"	60
	Lesson 14: Shared Reading of the Short Text, "Jane Goodall: A Portrait of Determination"	83
Drawing conclusions	Lesson 2: Partner Discussions of the Short Text, "Jorge Muñoz: An American Hero"	43
	Lesson 4: Partner Discussions Using the Text, "What Was Early Humans' Greatest Invention?"	51
	Lesson 8: Partner Discussions of the Short Text, "The Day I Started Becoming an American"	63
	Lesson 9: Partner Discussions of the Poem, "Ode to the Skunk"	66
	Lesson 10: Partner Discussions for the Text, "I Am Not a Number"	69
	Lesson 13: Shared Reading of the Poem, "The Man for the Job"	80
	Lesson 20: Shared Reading of the Short Text, "The Masters of Pollination"	103
Identifying author's purpose	Lesson 16: Shared Reading of the Short Text, "The Service Dog: Man's Best Friend"	90
Identifying literary elements	Lesson 17: Shared Reading of the Poem, "Lost and Found"	93
Identifying personality traits	Lesson 7: Partner Discussions of the Poem, "The Explorers"	60
	Lesson 19: Shared Reading of the Poem, "George Washington Carver"	100
Making connections	Lesson 2: Partner Discussions of the Short Text, "Jorge Muñoz: An American Hero"	43
	Lesson 6: Partner Discussions of the Short Narrative, "Manhunt"	57
Making inferences	Lesson 6: Partner Discussions of the Short Narrative, "Manhunt"	57
	Lesson 8: Partner Discussions of the Short Text, "The Day I Started Becoming an American"	63
	Lesson 9: Partner Discussions of the Poem, "Ode to the Skunk"	66
	Lesson 10: Partner Discussions for the Text, "I Am Not a Number"	69
	Lesson 12: Partner Discussions Using the Poem, "If Stones Had Tongues"	76
	Lesson 13: Shared Reading of the Poem, "The Man for the Job"	80

FOREWORD

Recent assessments of eighth grade reading achievement in the United States have not been encouraging. In the most recent National Assessment of Educational Progress (The Nation's Report Card, 2019) report, eighth grade reading achievement was largely the same as it was over 20 years ago. In 1998, the percentage of eight graders reading below a basic level was 27%. In 2019, the percentage reading below basic was exactly the same—27%. The percentage reading at *proficient* or *advanced* actually declined from 1998!

What's going on? We've been told that we need to rely more on the science of reading in developing curriculum and delivering instruction. In the middle grades, the science of reading suggests that a focus on vocabulary, fluency, and comprehension are appropriate. I agree fully. Middle grade students cannot comprehend a text well if they don't understand the words in the text; they will experience difficulty in comprehension if they are not fluent (effortless and expressive) in their reading; and certainly, they cannot comprehend what they read if they are not actively involved in making meaning as they read.

But this understanding of the science of reading has been known since the report of the National Reading Panel in 2000. Certainly, we should have expected some improvement over the next 19 years as schools and reading programs embraced the science of reading. And yet, we have barely even budged the needle.

While acknowledging the importance of science in teaching reading, we need to also recognize that teaching in general, and the teaching of reading, in particular, is also an art (Rasinski, 2019). Teachers need to be artists as well as scientists. We need to find ways of delivering scientifically based instruction in artful, engaging, and authentic ways.

Enter Laura Robb and David Harrison. Both are good friends of mine. More importantly, both are passionate literacy educators in their own ways. Laura is first and foremost a middle school teacher. She is also a scholar-author of several books on teaching reading in the middle grades. David's primary passion is as a poet (pardon the alliteration)—an award-winning poet. But he has also written professionally on the value of using poetic texts in the literacy curriculum. An interesting combination, wouldn't you say? A teacher who is also a scholarly author, and a poet who wants to improve literacy instruction in the classroom Yet, it is often combinations like these that can lead to remarkable results.

In their new book, Laura and David provide you with actionable and artful lessons for use in your classroom for what we now call *close reading*. What I truly love about the lessons is that they can be used as models for developing your own lessons. David actually provides with the relatively short text (canvas) for each lesson, and Laura provides you with the instructional brush strokes for helping students take a deep dive into vocabulary, fluency, comprehension, and writing. The appendix provides you with great resources for developing your own masterpiece lessons.

What excites me even more about this book is its emphasis on reading fluency through practice and performance (Part 3). My own research (Rasinski, 2010), as well the research of others (Rasinski, Reutzel, Chard, & Linan-Thompson, 2011), indicates that fluency is a critical instructional goal of reading through the middle grades and beyond (Paige, Rasinski, & Magpuri-Lavell, 2012, 2014; Rasinski et al., 2005; Rasinski, Rikli, & Johnston, 2009). And yet, it often suffers from benign neglect in many classrooms (Rasinski, 2012). As a result, we have many middle and secondary students who struggle in overall reading achievement in the middle and secondary grades (recall the 2019 NAEP results for Grade 8). Robb and Harrison provide you with instructional guidelines for providing students with opportunities to practice (rehearse) and perform, with expression and meaning, the wonderfully aesthetic texts that David Harrison has written.

There is so much to like about what Laura and David have written. After you read it, and try it out with your students, I hope you will agree that this book will help you understand better that the best reading instruction in the middle grades is both a science and an art.

Timothy Rasinski, PhD
Professor of Literacy Education
Rebecca Tolle and Burton W. Gorman Chair in Educational Leadership
Kent State University

REFERENCES

NAEP. (2019). *NAEP Report Card: Reading National*. The Nation's Report Card. Retrieved from https://www.nationsreportcard.gov/reading/nation/achievement/?grade=8

Paige, D. D., Rasinski, T. V., & Magpuri-Lavell, T. (2012). Is fluent, expressive reading important for high school readers? *Journal of Adolescent & Adult Literacy, 56(1)*, 67–76.

Paige, D. D., Rasinski, T. V., Magpuri-Lavell, T., & Smith, G. (2014). Interpreting the relationships among prosody, automaticity, accuracy and silent reading comprehension in secondary students. *Journal of Literacy Research, 46(2)*, 123–156.

Rasinski, T. (2010). *The fluent reader: Oral and silent reading strategies for building word recognition, fluency, and comprehension* (2nd ed.). New York, NY: Scholastic.

Rasinski, T. (2012). Why reading fluency should be hot. *The Reading Teacher, 65*, 516–522.

Rasinski, T. (2019). Teaching reading is an art as well as a science. *The Robb Review*. Retrieved from https://therobbreviewblog.com/uncategorized/teaching-reading-is-an-art-as-well-as-a-science/

Rasinski, T., Padak, N., McKeon, C., Krug-Wilfong, L., Friedauer, J., & Heim, P. (2005). Is reading fluency a key for successful high school reading? *Journal of Adolescent and Adult Literacy, 49*, 22–27.

Rasinski, T. V., Reutzel, C. R., Chard, D., & Linan-Thompson, S. (2011). Reading fluency. In M. L. Kamil, P. D. Pearson, B. Moje, & P. Afflerbach (Eds.), *Handbook of reading research, volume IV* (pp. 286–319). New York, NY: Routledge.

Rasinski, T., Rikli, A., & Johnston, S. (2009). Reading fluency: More than automaticity? More than a concern for the primary grades? *Literacy Research and Instruction, 48*, 350–361.

ACKNOWLEDGMENTS

From Laura Robb

My deepest thanks to three exemplary and skilled fifth grade teachers: Wanda Waters, Bridget Wilson, and Stacy Yost. Each one has used several of the guided practice lessons with their developing readers. Their feedback and unflagging dedication to support students have shaped the lessons in this book as well as let me know how much students enjoyed reading, discussing, and writing about the poems and short texts.

Thanks to award-winning poet, David Harrison, for his thoughtful collaboration as we both researched and then figured out topics that would appeal to middle grade and middle school students. How joyful for me to develop lessons using the engaging, motivating, and accessible poems and short prose texts that David wrote.

To Jennifer Harrison, my thanks for taking photographs and video of your students performing David's poems! Thanks, as well, to my son Evan Robb, a middle school principal and author, who read early drafts of the chapters and lessons and gave me invaluable feedback. And to Tori Bachman, my editor, who has my sincere thanks and appreciation for her depth of knowledge and her unique ability to communicate with authors. This book has developed over several months because of your outstanding insights, editing skill, and never-ending willingness to field my questions and provide valuable feedback.

And finally, my thanks to all the developing readers that have helped me see the need for guided practice lessons and provided valuable feedback by trying early iterations of the shared reading and partner discussion lessons.

From David L. Harrison

Now and then a teacher expresses appreciation (and, I think, surprise) for my grasp of what goes on in the classroom and the skill and dedication it takes to reach every student at his/her level of learning and support continued growth. Of course, I make no claim to be a scholar of education, but it has been my pleasure and honor for more than two decades to co-author books for the classroom with some of the most knowledgeable professors and teachers in education. Once again, I have been privileged to work with one of the best—Laura Robb. Laura, thank you. It has been a wonderful learning experience writing with you and watching you at work.

I also learned from the teachers in our book. I loved how you somehow made time for us when we came to you to "test drive" subject matter and activities. Laura has already named you so I add my gratitude here.

Tori Bachman, at last we got to work together. Hooray! And it was just the way I knew it would be—great! I've been impressed from first to last by the Corwin team. This, I believe, is a good book. And the result is in no small measure due to your caring and careful attention to detail every step of the way. My thanks to all.

PUBLISHERS ACKNOWLEDGMENTS

Corwin gratefully acknowledges the contributions of the following reviewers:

Dr. Carmen Gordillo
Rutgers University
Union City, NJ

Lynn Angus Ramos
DeKalb County School District
Decatur, GA

Judy Wallis
University of Houston
Houston, TX

PART 1

Why Guided Practice in the ELA Block

I've just completed five guided practice shared reading lessons with my group of sixth graders who are developing readers. I use the term *developing readers* instead of struggling or striving because I believe that all children, even those who are a grade level (or two, three, or more) below their peers, can develop into competent readers who enjoy reading at school and home! The hesitancy in students about participating I had noticed during the first two lessons recently transformed into full participation. I observed progress in using context to determine the meanings of tough words and students' ability to infer and visualize. It was time to hear their thoughts, so I grabbed a pencil and notebook and asked, "How have these lessons supported your reading?" I scribbled their answers, which surprisingly, rolled out like water cascading down a mountain:

- I felt good because if I got stuck, you'd ask a question to help me.

- Today, I was able to figure out "mercenary."

- It helped that we talked [to a partner] and then gave answers.

- I'm getting better at making inferences. I was scared the first time.

- I like that we [students] help each other.

Students' responses revealed how much they felt supported by peers and me. Knowing I wouldn't give an answer but would ask questions to stir their thinking, students told me that they had begun to have confidence in themselves as reading problem solvers. In addition, working together had firmed up their sense of community.

Guided practice lessons, an interim learning step sandwiched between a mini-lesson and instructional reading, is one way for students to engage in guided practice. Using a short text, students practice what their teacher modeled during the interactive read-aloud. Guided practice spotlights those students who can successfully apply a specific skill and those who require extra practice and support. The beauty and benefit of guided practice is that teachers can provide interventions before students dive into long texts. It's an opportunity to repair small confusions before they grow into large obstacles that can diminish students' progress and reading comprehension. The selections in this book are age-appropriate and on topics that motivate and build the background knowledge developing middle school readers need. When students learn with these texts, they not only improve their reading skill, but they also develop the social-emotional well-being that develops when they learn from the poems and short texts appropriate for their grades instead of having to read books written for students in K–2. Though you might feel that finding the time for guided practice is a challenge, know that these lessons can greatly improve the progress of developing to proficient readers in Grades 4–8 by improving their reading skill and developing the self-confidence they need to press forward and work hard.

So how do you find time for guided practice? Most Grade 4–8 teachers have a block of time from 45 to 60 minutes a day to teach reading and an extra 30 to 45 minutes for writing. I favor ELA classes that open with independent reading, followed by an interactive read-aloud or mini-lesson. Guided practice lessons using short texts are part of instructional reading. Most guided practice lessons last fifteen to thirty minutes over two to three days. The graphic in Figure 1.1 shows how guided practice fits into a 50-minute ELA class. If you have a 42- to 45-minute block, you'll only be able to complete guided practice and perhaps one conference.

FIGURE 1.1: GUIDED PRACTICE CAN BE ON ANY THREE CONSECUTIVE DAYS YOU CHOOSE.

Monday	Tuesday	Wednesday	Thursday	Friday
Independent reading: 15 minutes	Independent reading: 15 minutes	Independent reading: 15 minutes	Independent reading: 15 minutes	Independent reading: 15 minutes
Teacher reads aloud: 12 minutes	Teacher reads aloud: 12 minutes	Guided practice: 20 minutes	Guided practice: 30 minutes	Guided practice: 20 minutes
Instructional reading: 20 minutes	Instructional reading: 20 minutes	Teacher confers; students complete notebook writing or read		Teacher confers; students complete notebook writing or read
Wrap up	Wrap up	Wrap up	Wrap up	Wrap up

Appendixes A and B show ELA schedules for 45- and 60-minute class periods. Adapt the schedules to your specific needs and keep the guidelines fluid, as some days you'll spend more time on a task because that's what students need. Be flexible, for it's students who inform your instruction. Keep in mind that guided practice builds students' reading capacity and skill as long as the students do the reading, thinking, discussing, and writing.

There are no recipes or premade scripts when you teach this way. Readers' notebooks replace worksheets. Beautifully written and illustrated books relevant to students' lives and interests replace the class novel, a basal, or computer program. Reading volume matters, and students can boost their reading mileage and skill when they do the reading and problem solving on their own (Allington, 2002, 2012, 2014; Burkins & Yaris, 2018; Krashen, 2004). Your students are the script; their interests, abilities, and needs are the recipe. And the professional reading and conversations you have with colleagues about teaching and learning enable you to support the diverse learners in your classes. It's impossible for a pre-made program or one-size fits all scripted reading curriculum to know your students' unique needs. *Only you do!* And the guided practice reading lessons in this book can help you capitalize on your knowledge and relationships with the students you teach.

Readers' Notebooks Improve Comprehension

The research by Graham, Harris, and Santangelo (2015) makes a strong case for students writing about reading. The authors show that when students write about texts they can read, "their comprehension of that text jumps 24 percentile points." That's why having students write about reading should be an integral part of instructional reading lessons. Further, research shows that adults and students can only write what they understand (Murray, 1984; Self, 1987). So students' notebook writing is your window into their thinking processes, their comprehension, and their ability to use language to express ideas. Reading students' entries has a huge benefit; their writing informs your instructional decisions: to move on because students *get it*, to rewind and review, or re-teach.

Model how to respond in your notebook using your interactive read-aloud or another common text. Providing this mental model for students enables them to complete a task with understanding. See pages 26–27 for more on readers' notebooks.

CHAPTER 1

What Developing Readers Need

Independent reading needs to happen every day.

This day was a first for me! I had worked with students reading one to two years below grade level but never with students entering fifth grade reading from an early first to second grade level. Most had never read a book; they listened to teachers read books aloud and worked on computer reading programs. To bring these fifth graders into the reading life, I knew they had to read, read, read, because volume would be key to their progress. Even though teachers had a daily 60-minute ELA class, it wasn't enough time to change many students' reading trajectories because there were 24 students reading from kindergarten to sixth grade instructional levels.

To solve the problem of time, the fifth grade team at Daniel Morgan Intermediate School in Winchester, Virginia, lobbied for an extra class. In January, the district funded a daily 73-minute class for 24 students reading from an early first to beginning third grade level; Stacey Yost, Bridget Wilson, and I team-taught the class. During the 15–20 minutes of guided reading, I supported the six English language learners (ELL) students reading at a beginning first grade level. They had been in the school system since kindergarten and spoke English well. But they couldn't read.

At our first meeting, I asked the group, "How do you feel about reading?" No responses. I followed up with two questions: "Do you enjoy listening to teachers read aloud? Do you have a favorite book you've listened to?" Still, no one shared. Eyes focused on the table, they avoided looking at me. During the remaining time I started reading aloud, *I Can Be Anything! Don't Tell me I Can't* by Diane Dillon (2018). Students' silence, shrugging of shoulders, and quizzical looks when I asked them to share their dreams told me that their hopes-and-dreams tanks were on empty.

The next day, during guided reading I asked, "Why do you think it's important to learn how to read?" And Kendra blurted, "So others don't make fun of us!" Silence. Nods of agreement—a door had opened. Three of the six students shared their feelings that day. They talked about times they had to read aloud and classmates laughed as they stumbled through a short passage or times when they couldn't answer a question because they couldn't read and understand the material.

After each class Stacey, Bridget, and I discussed what we had learned from students. Most carried negative reading baggage and covered up their lack of progress by checking out, from the school's library and our class library, books they couldn't read. They were desperate to look like grade level readers and avoid the comments about having to read *baby* books from peers.

How to choose a *good fit* book was a lesson Stacey, Bridget, and I repeated several times a week. We took turns modeling for students (see box). Six weeks later, we noticed some students selecting books they could read and enjoy. We celebrated these changeovers and gave students the gift of time they needed to choose books they could read and enjoy.

How to Teach Students to Choose a *Good Fit* Book

- Think aloud and show what you feel and think when you choose a book that is too difficult: can't say many words, don't know many word meanings, and can't recall details.

- Think aloud to model how you know you've found a *good fit* book: it's easy to read, enjoyable, and you can retell.

- Keep modeling and emphasize that independent reading should be enjoyable.

- Reassure students that they are safe in your class and can select a book they can easily read. Explain that the more they read accessible books, the faster their reading will improve.

Daily, the three of us took turns sharing this mantra during guided reading and when we modeled how to choose a *good fit* book: *In this class you are safe. No one will make fun of you or criticize you. We are here to learn together and support one another.* It might seem like a small thing. But for these students who lived with failure for such a long time, we hoped that by repeating these words, combined with their reading successes, students' self-confidence and trust in our community would continually improve.

We became dedicated kid-watchers and listeners, eager to learn as much as we could about our developing readers (Owacki & Goodman, 2002). We met frequently to share literacy stories and what we noticed during daily interactive read-alouds. Observations of and conversations with students continually deepened our knowledge of their feelings and beliefs about learning to read.

CHARACTERISTICS OF DEVELOPING READERS IN MIDDLE GRADES

Year after year when students make little to no progress in reading, they can develop characteristics that prevent their growth and progress. Stacey, Bridget, and I identified ten characteristics based on the middle-grade developing readers we taught. These students:

- lack self-confidence
- feel embarrassed reading *easy books* in front of peers
- have difficulty decoding multi-syllable words
- choose challenging books so peers think they can read
- have learned the art of fake reading
- don't read at school or at home
- can't read grade-level materials and don't receive alternative materials
- have developed an "I can't do it" outlook
- become quiet, silent, and hope no one will call on them
- don't dream of what they want to be or do beyond school years

One of our goals was to teach students about the Power of Yet (Dweck, 2007), explaining that they might not be able to reach a goal *yet* today, but with practice, hard work, and our support, they could achieve it. During our bi-monthly study group, we discussed personal and collective efficacy, the belief that with skilled teaching we could reverse the pattern of little to no reading progress for these students (Donahoo, 2016). That year, the fifth grade team not only improved their teaching skill by learning from students, but they also made a commitment to professional learning and becoming evolving teachers who continually grow and improve their practice.

DEVELOPING READERS NEED SKILLED TEACHERS

Skilled teachers create an environment where choice and negotiation are daily options for students. In addition, they recognize the importance of ongoing professional learning as a powerful pathway to develop, adjust, and refine their theory of learning to make decisions that boost students' progress.

Skilled Teachers Observe Students Carefully

Watching and listening to students can deepen your understanding of what they do and don't comprehend as well as their ability to explain ideas to peers, follow directions, use independent work time well, be active listeners who respond to what peers say, and their level of engagement in a learning experience. The eight tools that follow enable you to see each student as a unique individual and deepen your knowledge of how each one communicates, works with a team, analyzes material, listens, connects ideas, and transfers learning to different situations.

Kidwatching: Be relentless with observing students during interactive read-alouds, guided practice, instructional reading, student-led paired and small group discussions, and independent reading of self-selected books. You can notice and note whether students are listening, participating in discussions, talking out of turn, have materials for a lesson, frequently get up to sharpen pencils, or ask for a bathroom pass.

Listening: Tune your ears to whole class, small group, and partner discussions, and learn how students express their ideas and cite text evidence to support their thinking. You'll also note how frequently they participate, whether they value diverse interpretations of texts, and how they react to peers who challenge their thinking.

Raising questions: Skilled teachers have a questioning mindset and wonder about students' motivation, attitudes toward learning, and book choices. They encourage students to pose questions about how and what they are learning, knowing that students' queries can make visible concerns and confusions.

Conferring: Short, scheduled conferences between the teacher and student can reveal attitudes toward reading, past experiences with reading, the amount of independent reading completed at home, and students' comprehension and recall.

Fifth grade teacher Stacey Yost uses conferences to maintain the momentum of reading, so a student who never completed a book reads an entire self-selected book. Each week, Stacey confers with the student about a section completed and closes the conference inviting the student to decide how many pages he/she can read by their next meeting (see Figure 1.2 for a glimpse at Stacey's notes). "Students choose the book and set their own pace and goal," she says, "and that invests them in the reading. Most of the time, the student exceeds his/her goal and that offers me an opportunity to celebrate success. A student's weekly goal rises as success continues. Once they experience the joy of completing a book, they're ready and eager to read another one."

Interacting: Even brief interactions that occur during daily read-alouds, or as you circulate around the room during independent reading and stop to answer a student's question or listen to a discussion, can deepen your knowledge of what students understand and whether they require extra support. It's also beneficial to chat with students during lunch and recess as the sum of your interactions can build positive relationships that in turn enable students to accept and/or seek your support.

Reading students' writing: What students write in notebooks reveals what they understand and recall from their reading (Barone & Taylor,

FIGURE 1.2: NOTICE HOW STACEY SCHEDULES FREQUENT MEETINGS TO HELP THE STUDENT COMPLETE THE BOOK.

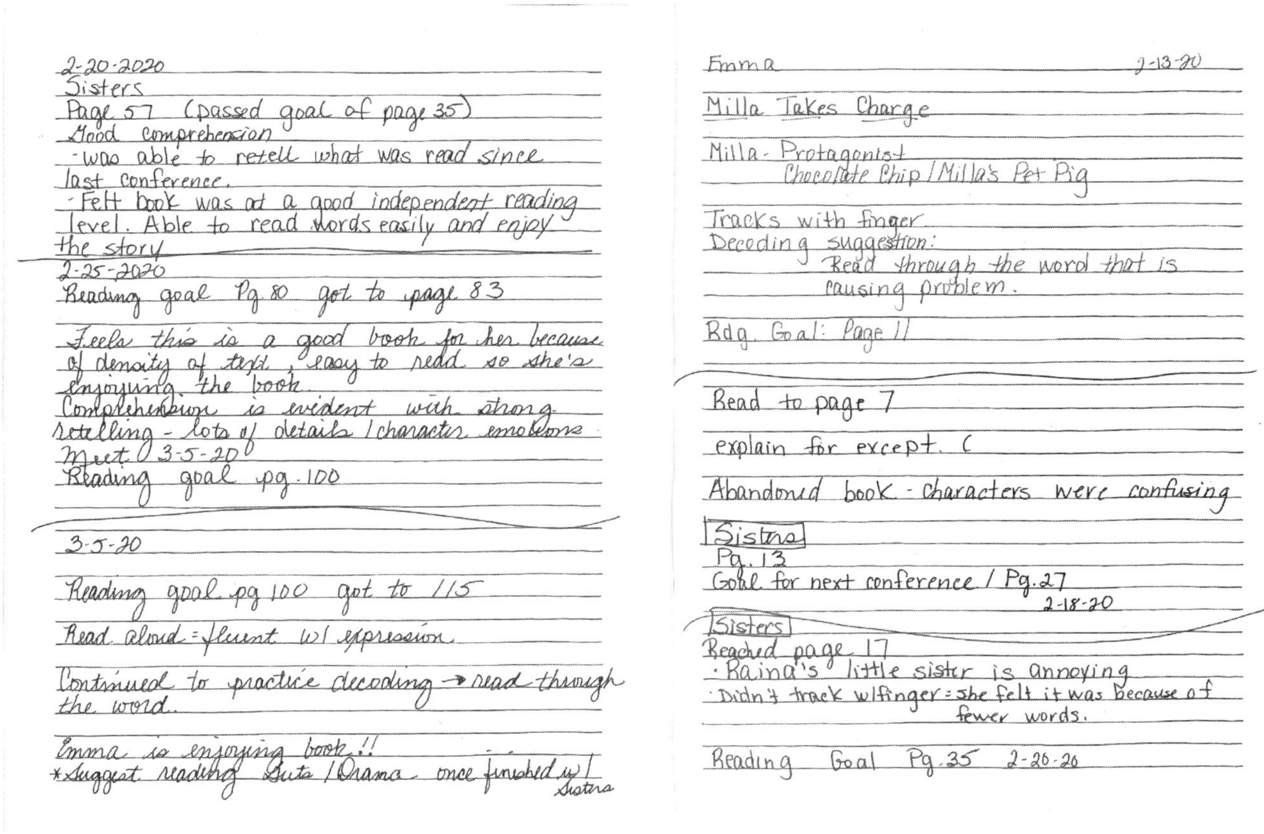

2-20-2020
Sisters
Page 57 (passed goal of page 35)
Good comprehension
- was able to retell what was read since last conference.
- Felt book was at a good independent reading level. Able to read words easily and enjoy the story
2-25-2020
Reading goal Pg. 80 got to page 83
Feels this is a good book for her because of density of text, easy to read so she's enjoying the book.
Comprehension is evident with strong retelling - lots of details / character emotions
Meet 3-5-20
Reading goal pg. 100

3-5-20
Reading goal pg 100 got to 115
Read aloud = fluent w/ expression.
Continued to practice decoding → read through the word.
Emma is enjoying book!!
*Suggest reading Guts / Drama once finished w/ Sisters

Emma 2-13-20
Milla Takes Charge
Milla - Protagonist
Chocolate Chip / Milla's Pet Pig
Tracks with finger
Decoding suggestion:
Read through the word that is causing problem.
Rdg. Goal: Page 11

Read to page 7
explain for except. (
Abandoned book - characters were confusing
Sisters
Pg. 13
Goal for next conference / Pg. 27
2-18-20
Sisters
Reached page 17
· Raina's little sister is annoying
· Didn't track w/finger = she felt it was because of fewer words.
Reading Goal Pg. 35 2-20-20

2006; Robb, 2017). Alana, a fifth grader in Wanda Waters's class, started the year by listing facts from a book. By March, her notebook entries showed her ability to identify a problem and its solution (See Figure 1.3).

Keeping a teacher's notebook: When students see you writing in a teacher's notebook, they develop a mental model of expectations for writing about reading. Your teacher's notebook can show them what a written response looks like. Most developing readers are also developing writers who need models for how to write about texts they listen to and read independently (see pages 25–26 for more information).

Seeking feedback from others: There will be times you'll want to discuss a student with a colleague, reading resource teacher, the school's media specialist, or guidance counselor. By inviting fresh eyes to review students' work and your kidwatching notes, you can gather intervention suggestions that didn't occur to you. Always ask for feedback when the support you're offering isn't working well or when you'd like to have extra ideas for intervening in reserve.

Teachers who continually refine and adjust these tools can transform developing readers into confident readers who choose to read at school and at home. Having a written record of your observations supports this goal as you weigh decisions about next steps for a student and target the kind of support you'll provide.

FIGURE 1.3: THE TEACHER MODELS PROBLEM SOLUTION (SEVERAL TIMES), AND THEN ALANA TRIES THE STRATEGY WITH HER INSTRUCTIONAL READING BOOK.

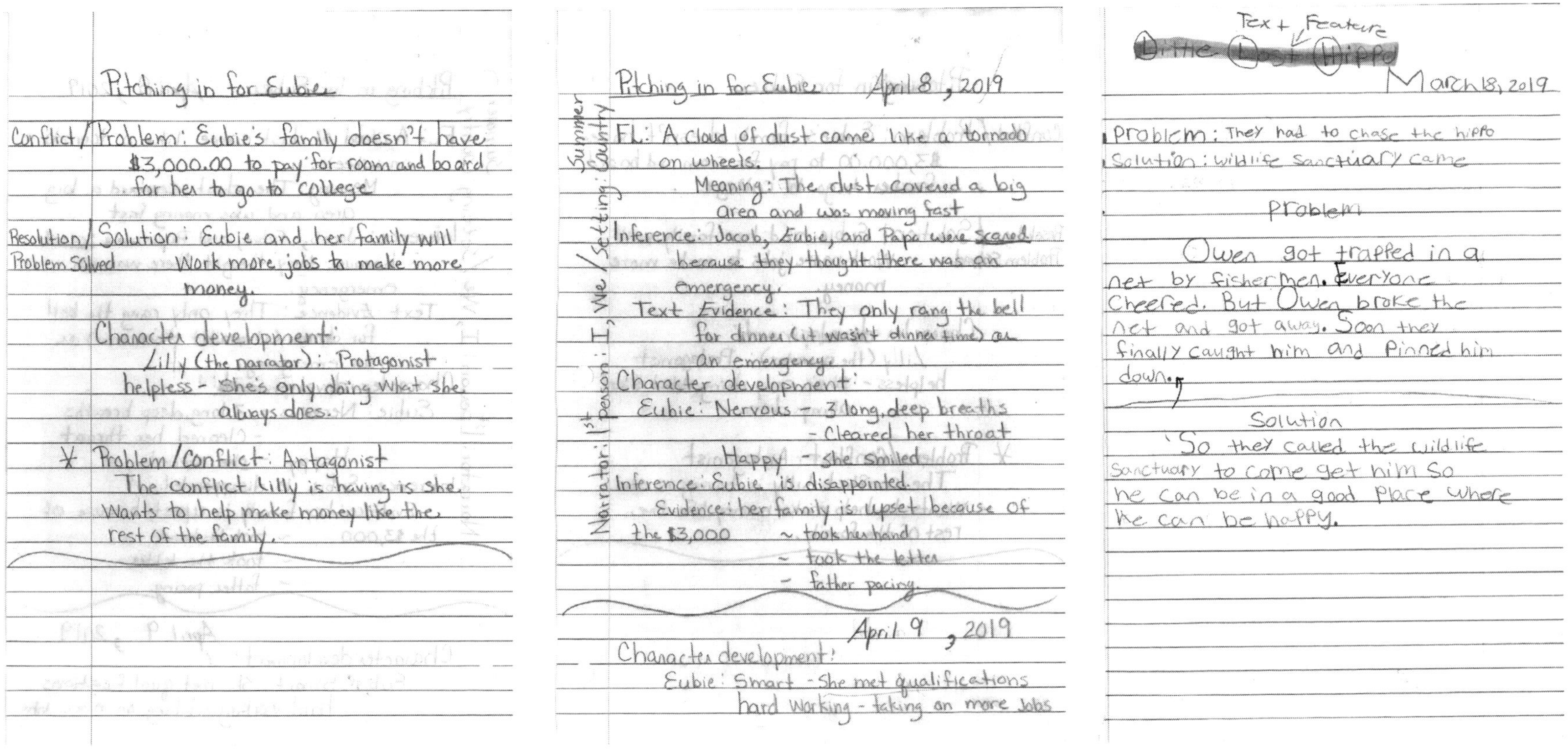

Tex + Features
The Lost Hippo   March 18, 2019

Problem: They had to chase the hippo
Solution: wildlife sanctuary came

Problem
Owen got trapped in a net by fishermen. Everyone cheered. But Owen broke the net and got away. Soon they finally caught him and pinned him down.

Solution
So they called the wildlife sanctuary to come get him so he can be in a good place where he can be happy.

Pitching in for Eubie   April 8, 2019

Summer / Setting: Country   We

FL: A cloud of dust came like a tornado on wheels.
Meaning: The dust covered a big area and was moving fast
Inference: Jacob, Eubie, and Pepe were scared because they thought there was an emergency.
Text Evidence: They only rang the bell for dinner (it wasn't dinner time) an emergency

Character development:
Eubie: Nervous - 3 long, deep breaths - cleared her throat

1st person / Narrator

Happy - she smiled
Inference: Eubie is disappointed
Evidence: her family is upset because of the $3,000   ~ took husband isn't
~ took the kitten
- father pacing

Character development: April 9, 2019
Eubie: Smart - she met qualifications
hard working - taking on more jobs

Pitching in for Eubie

Conflict/Problem: Eubie's family doesn't have $3,000.00 to pay for room and board for her to go to college

Resolution/Solution: Eubie and her family will work more jobs to make more money.
Problem Solved

Character development:
Lily (the narrator): Protagonist - helpless - she's only doing what she always does.

X Problem/Conflict: Antagonist
The conflict Lily is having is she wants to help make money like the rest of the family.

Skilled Teachers Take Notes to Help Differentiate Instruction

Early in my teaching career, I learned the importance of jotting notes to record my observations of students during daily interactive read-alouds and while students work independently, with a partner, or with me in a small group. Notes became my memory, and in conjunction with students' notebook writing, they offered information about students' progress. Notes help you make informed decisions about the instruction your students need, allowing you to differentiate with more confidence and impact. Moreover, notes can support recommendations during IEP (individual educational plans) meetings. Here are some tips for streamlining and organizing daily notes.

Notice and note: Place dated sticky notes on several sheets of blank paper and attach to a clipboard. Avoid editorializing and keep notes as objective as possible because you'll frequently find yourself sharing your notes with students during conferences. Figure 1.4 is an example of my notes for students after a guided practice lesson. Notice how I jot positives in addition to areas needing support. I do this to help students notice small increments of progress that they don't always see.

Storing daily notes: At the end of each day, transfer your notes into a loose-leaf binder or Google doc. Use dividers to separate the ELA sections you teach. In each section, note a student's name on about three sheets of paper—you can add more once you've filled the front and back of each sheet.

TEACHING TIP

Set aside time, every two to three weeks, to review the notes for each student. Start with students who aren't making enough progress and see if your notes offer clues for moving that child forward. For example, I noticed that fifth grader Jaylinda's poetry reading, at the end of each week, wasn't fluent and expressive, even though there was time for daily practice with a partner. A review of my notes revealed she had not read her poem to her partner during the last two weeks. Instead of making this a behavior issue, I observed Jaylinda and her partner every day for a week. When her fluency and expression improved, I conferred with her and discussed the benefits of daily practice. Having the notes pinpointed the issue and enabled me to design a positive intervention instead of calling attention to what she wasn't doing and risk enlarging her frustration and anger.

While working with developing readers, the temptation to move from mini-lessons to reading books is powerful. However, I have learned that it's best to slow down and invest in guided practice, so students can develop skill applying a strategy you've modeled during a mini-lesson. Having time to practice can improve students reading, writing, and discussions.

DEVELOPING READERS NEED FOUR KEY LITERACY EXPERIENCES

Guided practice lessons can nudge students forward quickly when they are part of a literacy rich classroom that values daily teacher read-alouds, instructional and independent reading, and notebook writing about reading. To move students forward quickly, you'll have to maintain a balance between:

- daily read-alouds, including interactive read-alouds;
- instructional reading that includes guided practice, small group instruction, or a workshop approach where students read different texts within a genre or topic;
- daily independent reading of self-selected books; and
- writing about reading in notebooks.

FIGURE 1.4: ROBB'S NOTES AFTER GUIDED PRACTICE ALWAYS HIGHLIGHT WHAT'S WORKING, AND SHE RAISES ONE POINT TO REFLECT ON FOR POSSIBLE INTERVENTION.

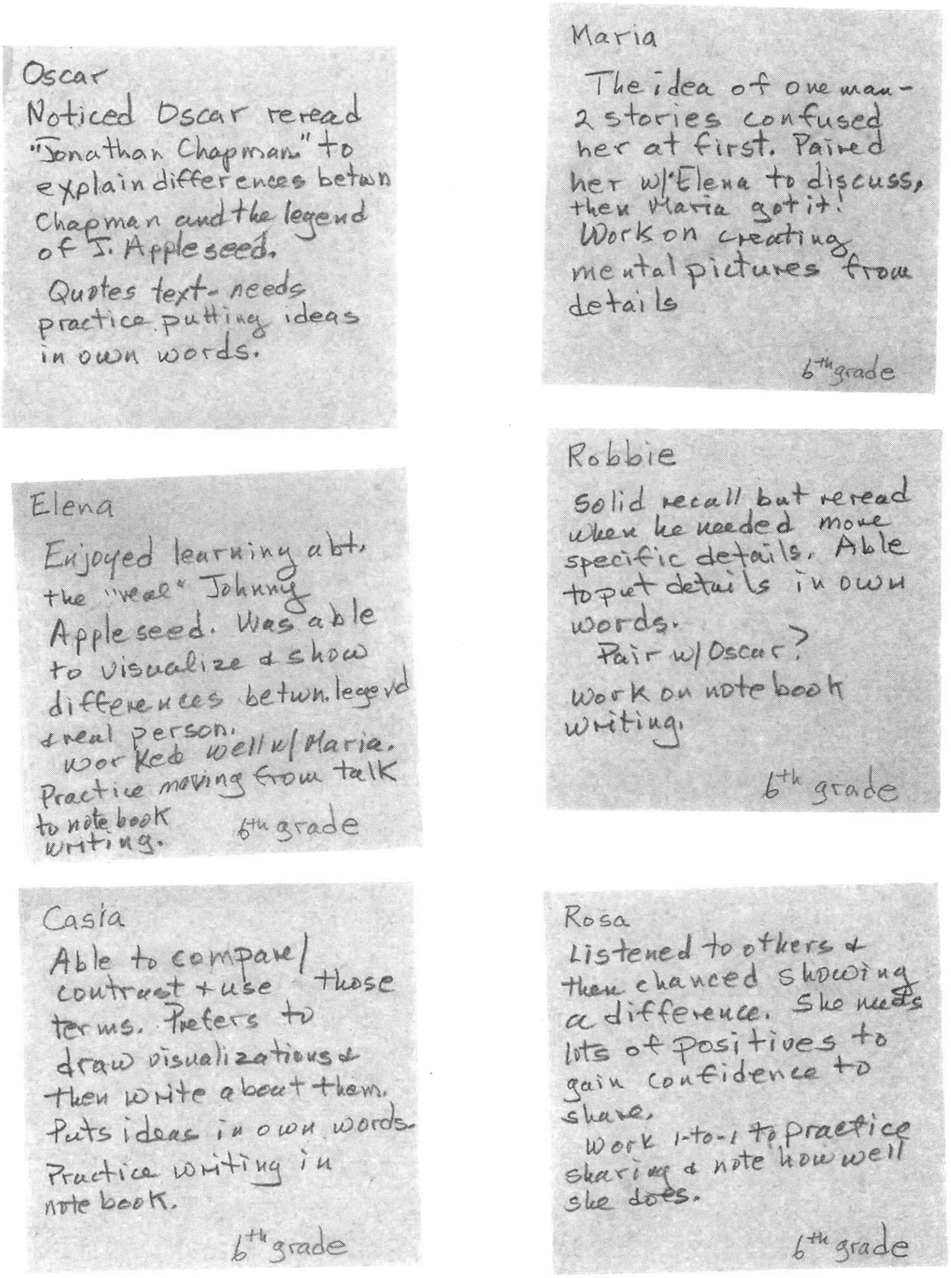

Oscar
Noticed Oscar reread "Jonathan Chapman" to explain differences betwn Chapman and the legend of J. Appleseed.
Quotes text- needs practice putting ideas in own words.

Maria
The idea of one man- 2 stories confused her at first. Paired her w/ Elena to discuss, then Maria got it! Work on creating mental pictures from details
6th grade

Elena
Enjoyed learning abt. the "real" Johnny Appleseed. Was able to visualize & show differences betwn. legend & real person. Worked well w/ Maria. Practice moving from talk to notebook writing.
6th grade

Robbie
Solid recall but reread when he needed more specific details. Able to put details in own words.
Pair w/ Oscar? Work on notebook writing.
6th grade

Casia
Able to compare/ contrast & use those terms. Prefers to draw visualizations & then write about them. Puts ideas in own words. Practice writing in notebook.
6th grade

Rosa
Listened to others & then changed showing a difference. She needs lots of positives to gain confidence to share.
Work 1-to-1 to practice sharing & note how well she does.
6th grade

This four-pronged approach allows you to read aloud to model expressive, fluent reading, enlarge students' vocabulary and background knowledge, and show students how good readers react to and think about texts. Independent reading offers students the practice they need (but often haven't had) to enjoy books they choose and want to read (Gambrell, Marinak, Brooker, & McCrea-Andrews, 2011). Finally, students who write about their reading can improve comprehension of a text by 24 percentile points (Graham, Harris, & Santangelo, 2015).

The texts David Harrison and I invite you to use for guided practice lessons are on topics that interest students in Grades 4 on up, but they also challenge their depth of thinking and enlarge their vocabulary and background knowledge. These students don't have lots of time to grow and improve as readers. By the end of eighth grade, they should be reading close to or on grade level. To support this ambitious goal, all four elements need to be part of your ELA block (see Appendix B for possible schedules).

The four elements, like a string quartet, make literacy music for developing (and all) readers because each element offers them the instruction and independent practice they need to become proficient readers.

TEACHING TIP

If the lessons students complete indicate there's not enough progress, it's important to provide support quickly so small confusions don't become obstacles to learning. Interventions can be working through lessons one-on-one, pairing a student with a classmate who *gets it*, or re-teaching using a new short poem or text from Appendix I or a text you choose. Appendix I provides additional original poems and short texts by David Harrison, and Appendixes H and J provide suggested sources for short texts, books, and poetry.

DEVELOPING READERS NEED GUIDED PRACTICE

Guided practice is instructional reading in which students practice with a short text independently or with a partner. Most guided practice lessons can be completed in 15 to 30 minutes. You'll discover whether students have absorbed what you've modeled in a mini-lesson or interactive read-aloud. It's the practice piece that lets you know students' level of understanding, their use of vocabulary and background knowledge to improve recall and comprehension, and their ability to discuss using text evidence. Your careful observation of students during guided practice helps you decide on instructional moves that improve students' application of a strategy or completing a task on their own. By basing interventions on how students navigate a short text you can decide to:

- Confer with a student to deepen your understanding of his/her work.

- Have the student redo parts of the guided practice while you observe and help.

- Support a student or small group by asking them to explain their thinking and then think aloud to model how you would respond. Gradually release the responsibility for rethinking and adjusting responses to students.

- Pair-up students and ask them to support one another as they rethink and redo parts of their work.

First, take the time to analyze the results of a shared reading lesson and/or students' independent or paired guided practice. This information enables you to intervene to bring all students to a level of understanding that allows them to experience success when reading a book at their instructional level. The guided practice lessons in this book use poems and short fiction and nonfiction texts written by award winning author and poet, David Harrison. These poems and short texts introduce your developing reader to outstanding, beautifully written literature on topics of interest to students their age. In other words, your developing readers won't feel embarrassed about reading *baby books* or be bored by the subject matter.

DEVELOPING READERS NEED TO EXPERIENCE THE BENEFITS OF REREADING

For several months, I worked with a group of seventh grade English language learners. During the first week with these students, I discovered that they had never read a book or used a reader's notebook. Instead, these students read short texts on the front and back of 6 × 8 cards and completed a fill-in-the-blank or multiple-choice worksheet relating to the selection. They never reread parts of the short text if they were unsure of how to answer a question. Their progress, understandably, was limited because they weren't reading enough. Based on their experiences, they described reading as *boring* and *pointless*.

The first time I introduced rereading using a think-aloud to spotlight my confusion of a section of a *The First Step: How One Girl Put Segregation on Trial* (by Susan E. Goodman, illustrated by E. B. Lewis), a student blurted out, "Just skip it." Lots of nods from others let me know that rereading was not a strategy they used, nor did they understand its benefits. I continued and then pointed out how I could better understand the passage after rereading. While thinking aloud with different read-alouds, students practiced with me when we worked together on a common text. Each day, we'd read a common text and reread a confusing part or reread a few sentences to figure out the meaning of an unfamiliar word or re-enjoy a funny or moving part. I also explained, many times, that the good readers in their classes valued and used rereading.

Proficient and advanced readers continually use rereading to savor favorite parts of texts, to clarify meaning, and improve recall and comprehension. The guided practice lessons in this book invite students to choral or independently whisper read selections or read silently along with you as well as reread pieces to develop fluency and deepen their comprehension of vocabulary and information. When developing readers continually practice reading and rereading, they begin to read with the fluency and expression, which signal understanding and depth of comprehension.

DEVELOPING READERS
NEED TO TALK ABOUT TEXTS

Student partners discuss pictures and text to deepen comprehension.

Many developing readers have not had opportunities to read and discuss books with a partner or in a small group. Even if they've listened to teachers read books aloud, there's no guarantee that they were listening and remembering. An ideal time to model how to talk about reading is during daily read-alouds and small group instruction. For example, you can talk about literary elements (see Appendix C), your feelings, and the text structures of informational books such as compare/contrast, cause/effect, and problem solution (Allington & Johnston, 2002; Garas-York & Almasi, 2017; Robb, 2017).

Using the picture book *Free As A Bird: The Story of Malala* by Lina Maslo as a text, I've included examples in italics of the kinds of text-focused talk I model for students. These are examples you can adapt and refine as you plan think-alouds based on a read-aloud or when discussing a common book with small groups:

The protagonist and problems: *I know Malala will have problems growing up in Pakistan when people say after her birth, "What bad luck." This makes me think that adults see girls as second rate, and it's better to have boy babies.*

Feelings the book raised: *I felt sad when Malala realizes women didn't have the same rights as men. She was supposed to marry early and have children. If she had dreams of what she wanted to be, she most likely couldn't achieve them.*

Decisions made: *Malala's father encouraged her to be free and follow her dreams. She attended school and won public speaking contests. The Taliban threatened her life when Malala decided to talk about education for girls. She continued to attend school even though it was dangerous.*

Antagonists' role: *The Taliban threats made Malala want to go to school and keep talking about her belief in education for girls. Their threats and the thought of not being able to go to schools gave her strength to speak out.*

Outcomes: *The enemy shot Malala, but she recovered in England. Once Malala was well, she became an activist, speaking out for equality and education for girls around the world.*

Changes in the protagonist: *Malala did not accept the traditional role for Pashtun girls. Instead, she spoke out for girls in her country and continues to speak out all over the world. She developed boundless courage and the belief that education and learning was a right for boys and girls.*

Settings: *The book starts in Pakistan to show a girl's position in Pashtun society and what Malala fought against. It also shows her father's and mother's support for Malala to achieve her dream of being educated.*

Cause/Effect: **Cause:** *The government and enemy fired guns at each other.* **Effect:** *Malala and her brothers hid in their parents' bedroom. Secretly, Malala continues to go to school.*

Encourage students to *notice* what your response showed to ensure they understand your thinking. Most likely, you'll be met with silence the first few times you do this. That's okay, as talking about a text is new territory for these students. Continue to think-aloud, explain your response, and eventually, students will join the *noticing* conversations.

TIME TO REFLECT

Reserve time to mull over what you've read in this chapter. Discuss the questions that follow with yourself or a colleague who is also reading this book.

- How do guided practice lessons improve developing readers?
- Why is it important for students to do the lion's share of the work?
- Why are kid-watching and taking observational notes important to student's progress?

CHAPTER 2

Organizing for Guided Practice

Students are deeply into their daily independent reading.

"But what will I teach?" A veteran teacher asked this question while we discussed moving from a teacher-centered to a student-centered approach. Her years of teaching a basal program with worksheets and unit tests had removed the necessity of creating experiences for students by responding to their needs. In addition, she had not read many professional books, nor did she feel professional learning would help her. "I follow the teacher's guide for the basal," she told me, "that's all I need."

However, a new superintendent for her district turned teachers' basal reading program world upside-down. He wanted ELA teachers to develop a workshop model and student-centered approach. Funding was set aside for individual schools to purchase professional materials for book and article studies. My job as a coach-consultant was to support teachers through conversations and workshop sessions inviting them to learn just as their students would learn. By the end of three years, everyone had moved to a student-centered workshop.

Now, teachers' 60-minute reading blocks opened with 15 minutes of students reading self-selected books from well-stocked class libraries to ensure that independent reading occurred daily. Once teachers understood the huge benefits of independent reading to students' reading progress, it became the constant of every English Language Arts (ELA) class. Guided practice and independent reading support one another. During guided practice, students work with you to use context clues to enlarge their vocabulary, discuss multiple forms of words, as well as build background knowledge. Students also apply reading strategies such as inferring and drawing conclusions during guided practice. Daily independent reading provides opportunities for students to use what they've learned during guided practice and link it to easier texts they select and can read. It's the additional practice students need to improve reading skill.

Balanced literacy was teachers' instructional organizer, and reading workshop also included student-led discussions, instructional reading, writing about reading in notebooks, book talks, author studies, and student-suggested projects. In addition, teachers added guided practice lessons using short texts. Taking this step enabled teachers to improve students' reading skill and identify students who could apply skills taught in a mini-lesson as well as pinpoint those who required extra support.

It's important to remember that guided practice is one piece of instructional reading that can nudge students forward. Combined with daily independent reading, it holds the potential of improving students' fluency, enlarging their vocabulary, and developing the self-confidence and skill needed to experience pleasure in reading books they choose. Guided practice can benefit readers at all levels but especially your developing readers. And it fits into a student-centered reading workshop approach because guided practice scaffolds learners to higher levels of comprehension, fluency, and enjoyment of reading. Our ultimate goal for developing readers is reading independently at grade level. To accomplish this, the guided practice lessons ask you to assess students' progress and decide whether they can move forward or would benefit from interventions such as reviewing or re-teaching.

In this chapter, you'll look closely at some of the most important learning experiences in a reading block that can help all students—but especially your developing readers—make gains in reading. You'll explore the benefits of independent reading, interactive read-alouds, vocabulary building, and writing about texts in reader's notebooks, so you can see how these teaching and learning experiences support guided practice and students' growth in reading.

INDEPENDENT READING
INCREASES VOLUME

A group of middle school teachers and I discuss reorganizing their reading block for the new school year. "I know independent reading is important," Mr. Davis says, "but it's the first thing that goes when I'm in a time crunch." Mr. Davis isn't alone. Finding time for independent reading is an issue for many teachers. However once you review the research on independent reading below, I believe it will become a top priority.

First, it's important to understand that reading volume matters, and the best way to increase students' reading mileage is through independent reading. By developing a love of reading at school, students are more likely to choose to read at home. Yet, teachers often tell me that their principals view students' reading during class as a poor use of instructional time. Here's the advice to administrators that researcher Stephen Krashen offers (2004):

> Administrators need to know that when teachers are reading to students, and when teachers are relaxing with a good book during sustained silent reading sessions, teachers are doing their job. Administrators need to know that a print-rich environment is not a luxury, but a necessity. (p. 151)

In addition to Stephen Krashen, Richard Allington (2002, 2012, 2014), in his landmark 1977 article, "If they don't read much, how are they gonna get good?" has been extolling the need for volume in reading for all students, but especially for developing readers.

Anderson, Wilson, and Fielding (1988) conducted research on the value of independent reading. Though the National Reading Panel did not consider their study scientific, Dr. S. Jay Samuels and Dr. Yi-Chen Wu (2004) completed a scientific study in response to the National Reading Panel. Their study showed that the more time students spent reading, the higher their achievement compared to a control condition. Both researchers found that developing readers tended to have greater gains in vocabulary, reading speed, and comprehension with 15 minutes of independent reading but better gains in word recognition skills with 40 minutes of reading. For proficient and advanced readers, the study concluded that 40 minutes of independent reading a day "had the most beneficial effects for developing comprehension skills" (p. 20).

Based on these findings, the researchers recommend that the amount of time assigned to independent reading should match students' reading ability. My recommendation is that as students develop reading skill and stamina, they can and should increase the amount of time they read.

The Samuels and Wu (2004) study closes with this conclusion:

> In conclusion, to answer the National Reading Panel report indicating that experimental experience is not available to answer the question about the relationship between time spent on reading and reading outcomes, this experimental study found that time spent reading independently interact with students reading ability and had a positive impact on certain components of reading achievement. (p. 20)

FIGURE 2.1: VARIATION IN AMOUNT OF INDEPENDENT READING

Percentile Rank for Reading Volume	Minutes a Day	Words a Year
98th	67.3	4,733,000
90th	33.4	2,375,000
70th	16.9	1,168,000
50th	9.2	601,000
30th	4.3	251,000
10th	1.0	51,000
2nd	0.0	_____

Source: Anderson, R., Wilson, P. & Fielding, L. (1988). "Growth in reading and how children spend their time outside school." *Reading Research Quarterly*, 3(23).

The chart in Figure 2.1 shows the relationship between time spent each day on independent reading and the number of words students read. Based on teachers' observations and experiences, independent reading also builds students' background knowledge and stamina, which is the ability to concentrate on reading 30 to 60 minutes. Moreover, reading volume develops students' literary tastes, deepens their understanding of different genres, and enlarges their vocabulary as they continually meet words used in different contexts over time.

In Chapter 1, I discussed what teachers can do to model how to choose a *good fit* book for developing readers, a book to read and enjoy on their own. Along with your modeling, it's helpful to write, on large chart paper, what students can do to find a book they'll enjoy. When you introduce this chart, developing readers will need to observe you model the suggestions many times.

Tips for Students: Selecting a *Good Fit* Book

- Look for books on topics and genres that interest you.

- Study the front cover illustration and read the information on the back cover or the inside cover flap. Do you want to open the book and read? Why?

- Think of books you've read and enjoyed. Is the topic, genre, or author similar?

- Read and enjoy the illustrations or photographs and gather information from them.

- Ask a friend to recommend a book he/she couldn't put down.

- Ask your teacher to recommend a book.

- Read the chapter titles in the table of contents and ask yourself, *Does this interest me? Do I know something about this topic? How do I feel about these ideas?*

- Take a test drive and read two to three pages or the first chapter. Did you want to read more? Was the reading enjoyable and easy?

Once students can select *good fit* books, invite them to explain to their peers their selection process. To change an entrenched habit of choosing books that look hard, books students can't read, you'll continually refresh students' memories of what's on the chart. The changeover will happen for students at different times, and periodic reminders of the selecting process can help them find books. Independent reading is the big game changer (Miller & Sharp, 2018). In addition, teachers who read aloud every day offer their students another powerful way to bond to stories and enlarge reading capacity.

DAILY INTERACTIVE READ-ALOUDS BENEFIT ALL READERS

When I arrived at a middle school in the Midwest, the principal told me I'd be working with students who "hated reading and didn't complete daily assignments." I shoved this negative message aside, walked into the class, introduced myself, and began reading "The Elevator," a short story by William Sleator. By the time I finished the second page, students had become silent; they were listening. When I stopped reading and said, "More tomorrow," these words echoed around the class: "Don't stop!" "Read more!" And I completed the story, following my feelings instead of my plan to complete the story in three consecutive classes. Students were invested and engaged, and it was more important to respond to their request than stick to my plans.

Fifth-grade teacher, Stacey Yost, engages her students in an interactive read-aloud.

When I finished reading the story, students speculated about what they thought the fat lady did to Martin, the protagonist: "She squeezed the breath outa him!" "Maybe it's all in his head." "Bet she tortured him." Sleator's story captured students' imagination. Now, my challenge was to sustain their enthusiasm through the lesson. During the remaining time, small groups of students read and discussed poems from *Love to Langston* by Tony Medina (2006)—poems portraying painful and powerful moments in the life of Langston Hughes. As I gathered my materials and started for the door, one student asked, "You got any more stories like that?"

"Sure do," I replied, "Make sure you're here tomorrow." I frequently replay this snapshot in my head and share it with teachers, for it shouts, loud and clear, the power of reading aloud stories that resonate with students.

The best follow-up to independent reading is the teacher reading aloud. Know your students and select picture books, short texts, and books that will resonate with them and touch their heads and hearts. Read a variety of genres so students learn the differences between historical fiction, fantasy, biography, and informational text.

Value recommendations from colleagues and your PLN (personal learning network), but *always* read the text yourself to ensure it's ideal for you and your students. I want you to love the books you read aloud to students because only with that mindset will you be able to transmit powerful feelings to them.

Daily interactive read-alouds can nurture a positive relationship between you and your students, bond them to stories and authors, and open doors to new experiences. The 10 reasons to read aloud every day listed below shine the spotlight on how this learning experience supports literacy and brings students into the reading life. When teachers read aloud, students:

1. **Learn how stories work** and develop a knowledge of literary elements (see Appendix C) that help them navigate fiction.

2. **Hear literary language** and tune their ears to complex sentences, rich and varied vocabulary, figures of speech, idioms, poetic description, and literary devices such as foreshadowing and irony.

3. **Develop their imagination** by visualizing characters, settings, and events and experiencing the emotions situations raise.

4. **Improve their cultural sensitivity.** As teachers read stories that celebrate diverse cultures, students can step into characters' shoes and experience their lives.

5. **Develop empathy and compassion** for beloved characters by experiencing their emotions, hopes, dreams, and challenges.

6. **Enlarge their vocabulary** by listening to the same words the author uses in different contexts. They also hear multiple forms of words and benefit from teachers introducing challenging words before the read-aloud starts.

7. **Increase listening capacity** and recall of chunks of text read each day. When students listen and remember, they can access text details they heard yesterday or a few days ago and apply them to a new situation.

8. **Nurture curiosity** by asking questions about a chunk of text and by making predictions, then listening to more of the story to adjust or confirm hunches.

9. **Build a positive connection to books** and reading every time they enjoy a story and connect to the characters, settings, and plot.

10. **Visit past, present, and future worlds** by listening to historical, realistic, and science fiction to explore time periods and connect to characters' lives.

Interactive read-alouds are a teaching tool that allow you, the expert reader in the class, to make visible to students the feelings a book raises in your heart, how you apply a strategy such as inferring, and the process you use for figuring out the meaning of unfamiliar words. I recommend you use picture books and spread your interactive read-aloud over four to five days. Moreover, developing readers can learn to infer, draw conclusions, and compare and contrast by discussing the illustrations in a book (Bryan, 2018). Learning to think at high levels using illustrations or photographs can boost students' self-confidence and enable them to apply the same strategies to the text. Because the interactive read-aloud is a teaching text, it's important to invest time and carefully prepare the lessons.

Preparing Interactive Read-Alouds

In addition to selecting a book that is the same genre and theme as your reading unit, you'll also prepare an anchor chart to pre-teach vocabulary, model a specific response, and note students' ideas after you've modeled. Below are suggestions for preparing a dynamic interactive read-aloud:

- Choose a picture book you enjoyed, read and reread it, and reflect on what you'll teach. Instead of diving into a strategy that students have struggled with in the past, first share the feelings the story raises within you as all readers can relate to emotions. Illustrations are an ideal starting point for discussing feelings.

- Divide the book into four to five chunks of text. Place a small sticky note at the top of the page that marks the end of a chunk and jot on the note, "Stop 1, Stop 2, Stop 3, etc." Choose stopping points that leave students begging you to read more or cause them to wonder what will happen next or what a character will do.

- Select one to two vocabulary words for each chunk. On the anchor chart, use each word in a sentence with strong context clues that help students understand the word as it's used in the text. This way, students discuss the word using your original sentence and then meet it again to discuss in the text. To enlarge students' vocabulary, under the sentence, note other forms of the word and discuss with students. For example, when reading aloud *Free as a Bird*, I introduce the word *disapproval* in the first chunk. Under my sentence, I write: *disapprove*, *disapproved*, *disapproving* (see Figure 2.2).

FIGURE 2.2: THE ANCHOR CHART FOR *FREE AS A BIRD* REVEALS THE WORD WORK AND THINKING THAT STUDENTS DO.

Anchor Chart
Free As a Bird: The Story of Malala
disapproval: When Jim spilled his lunch tray, his teacher's face showed disapproval. disaprove disapproved disapproving

Inference	Text Evidence
1. Women were 2nd class citizens.	1. Could not be what they wanted; had set role-marry-children
2. Father went against traditions.	2. Let Malala go to school, give speeches, dream of her goals.
3. Malala had great courage.	3. She secretly went to school. Enemy: girls couldn't go to school.
4. Malala had no fear. and lots of determination	4. "No one will stop me. I will get an education."
5. Taking a stand against injustice can change the world.	5. Gave speeches about how important it was for girls to go to school- even after she was wounded badly

Symbol Symbolism

6. red, black to blue	6. blood, death → life, peace
7. Malala symbolizes equality	7. girls + boys-education, life choices

- Raise questions. On a sticky note, write questions for each chunk of text and place each sticky note on its page; these are reminders while you read aloud. Questions should focus on the strategy you're modeling as well as emotional reactions.

- Set up the anchor chart for what you'll model for students. For example, for making inferences, I use a T-chart organizer. On the left hand side, I write: "Inference;" and on the right hand side, I write: "Text Evidence." (See Figure 2.2, completed anchor chart for *Free As a Bird*.)

Presenting Your Interactive Read-Aloud

While reading, you can show the text to students using a document camera or walk around the class so everyone can see the page. On the first day, show students the front and back cover, read the title, and have them turn-and-talk. Ask students: *What do you notice about the cover? How does it make you feel? What are you thinking when you see it?* Keep the questions open-ended and ask students to explain what in the cover illustration supports their noticing. Here's what sixth grade students said:

- "She wants to be free. The birds on back cover and the title helped me."

- "She likes reading—holds a book."

- "Her eyes look sad—maybe something bad happens."

- "Lots of red—the book, scarf, body of bird."

Using the cover illustrations, students have begun to draw conclusions. Next, show them the end papers, the title, and the copyright pages. Opening with illustrations is a positive way to front load students with some background knowledge and celebrate their thinking.

Now, begin reading the first chunk. For example, think aloud on the first two pages, then invite students to apply the same strategy you've modeled using a new page.

TEACHING TIP

By repeating the pattern and rhythm of your interactive read-alouds, developing readers have a road map for navigating the lessons and listening. Make sure that you continually revisit sets of words to strengthen students' vocabulary.

If students don't respond, return to thinking aloud. Be patient, as it takes time for students to process your modeling and stockpile enough self-confidence to offer ideas and text support. And remember, you want students to do the thinking as often as possible; resist the urge to jump in with answers. Make sure you jot students' responses on the anchor chart, as the chart becomes a resource and reminder for discussions and notebook writing when students read their own books. Repeat this pattern each time you read a chunk.

VOCABULARY INSTRUCTION INCREASES FLUENCY AND COMPREHENSION: TEACH WORDS IN GROUPS

The recommendation to teach words in groups makes sense for developing readers and all learners. Here's why: When you introduce and/or have students generate multiple related words, you show them connections among the words. At the same time you expand their vocabulary when you revisit the words and use them when speaking and thinking aloud. Once is never enough with vocabulary instruction. Repetition, helping students understand the words' meanings, and identifying how words work in reading materials and sentences you compose can move vocabulary learning from "these words seem familiar" to "I can communicate thoughts and ideas with these words."

In addition, those students who read independently and at school, steadily ramping up reading mileage, have large diverse vocabularies and background knowledge to bring to their reading (Beck, McKeown, & Kucan, 2013; Blachowicz & Fisher, 2006). Because developing readers don't read much, their vocabularies need boosting! To close the vocabulary gap among developing readers in Grades 4 and up, you need to introduce them to groups of words in the context of their reading. The more words students understand, the better their reading comprehension, the more choices of what to read they have, and their reading skill steadily moves forward.

Research shows a strong correlation between students' vocabulary and their reading comprehension. In 2009, NAEP (National Assessment of Educational Progress), the nation's report card, began a systematic study measuring the relationship between vocabulary knowledge and reading comprehension. In 2011, the NAEP results that compared vocabulary performance and reading comprehension showed a strong correlation between word knowledge and reading comprehension for students in Grades 4 and 8. That's why enlarging students' reading, thinking, and writing vocabulary is an important part of the guided practice lessons.

Here's the challenge that teachers face: How to enlarge students' vocabulary and at the same time improve their skill to the point they look forward to self-selected independent reading at school and home. Daily read-alouds, independent reading, guided practice, and instructional reading not only provide students with much needed practice, but they also allow you to build students' world knowledge. Avoid "the word of the day" and vocabulary workbooks. Instead, always teach words in related groups to increase students' vocabulary and cultivate an interest in words. Students learn words best when the words relate to books you and they read as well as the topics they're studying in all subjects. For example, with guided practice, if students use context to understand *survivor*, introduce them to the base word *survive* as well as *survived*, *surviving*, and *survival*.

TEACHING TIP

On your word wall and anchor charts, post groups of related words to nurture vocabulary growth. For example: relate, related, relating, relationship, relative, relatable.

Discuss related words, use them during your lessons, and expose students to 20 or more words every week. You'll increase their word knowledge as you:

- connect words to students' reading,
- use context to determine meaning,
- deepen students' knowledge of concepts,
- develop a curiosity about and interest in words, and
- show how different forms of words function in sentences.

Teaching words should relate to your curriculum, but there are three word-learning strategies students can practice that apply to what they're learning and the tasks they complete in all subjects.

1) **Teach words used in directions** so students can succeed with writing notebook entries and stories, taking quizzes and tests, completing projects, and communicating ideas while working on a team. Discussing the words that follow enables students to understand expectations:

   Example: define, evaluate, support, explain, categorize, conclude, defend, compare/contrast, show, sort, analyze, combine, revise, edit, identify, brainstorm

2) **Teach prefixes** such as *re* because they change words' meanings. Invite students to build sets of words that start with a specific prefix (see Figure 2.3).

   Example: rebuild, recall, reflect, redo, recharge, regain, refine, respect, reconnect, reread, rewrite, reseal, retry, reboot, revisit, remind

3) **Teach words describing personality traits** and help students move from *nice*, *kind*, and *sad* to more specific adjectives that show what a character or person is like. On chart paper, list banned words, so students can look for them as they revise their writing.

   Example: Instead of *kind* try helpful, compassionate, generous, supportive, understanding, sympathetic, thoughtful, considerate, concerned, sensitive, and good-natured.

In addition to playing with sets of words to enlarge students' vocabulary, keep a teacher's notebook so you can make visible how you think about words and texts and write notebook entries.

FIGURE 2.3: TEN COMMON PREFIXES

Prefix	Meaning	Example
un	not	unable
dis	apart, not, opposite of	disappear
in, im	in, into, not	indefinite
re	again, back	rebuild
pre	before, in front of	preview
sub	under	submarine
anti	against	antislavery
non	not	nonhuman
trans	across, beyond	transcribe
en, em	put, go into; to cause to be	endear, embed

TEACHERS' NOTEBOOKS MODEL WRITING ABOUT READING

By keeping a teacher's notebook, you have a place to model for students how to set up and organize a notebook page and how to write a range of responses to reading. For example, developing readers who have done little authentic writing and used worksheets might not know how to organize a double entry, question/answer, or compare/contrast response. Your notebook also documents mini-lessons you've presented, writing about reading, building groups of words, explaining a tough word using context clues—in other words, it's also a record of what you've modeled and taught. Having such a record allows you to return to a lesson and remind students what they've practiced prior to asking them to work independently. It is a teaching tool that benefits you and your students.

To model notebook writing for students, use the interactive read-aloud that is the common text for a unit when students read different books. Though some teachers find this suggestion challenging, it's helpful to cold write in front of students and think aloud so they observe the writing process and watch you talk about ideas and change words and phrases. Remember, developing readers have had limited experiences with the writing process. When you cold write you can demonstrate how you infer; compare/contrast; identify cause/effect; show changes in characters' personality traits; pinpoint themes and text structures; define words using context; and so forth. Figures 2.4 and 2.5 show examples from teachers' journals kept by Stacey Yost and Wanda Waters, respectively.

FIGURE 2.4: BRIDGET USES HER TEACHER'S NOTEBOOK TO MODEL HOW TO IDENTIFY A CHARACTER'S TRAITS USING THE PICTURE BOOK, *PITCHING IN FOR EUBI* BY JERDINE NOLEN, ILLUSTRATOR, E. B. LEWIS (JERDINE, 2007).

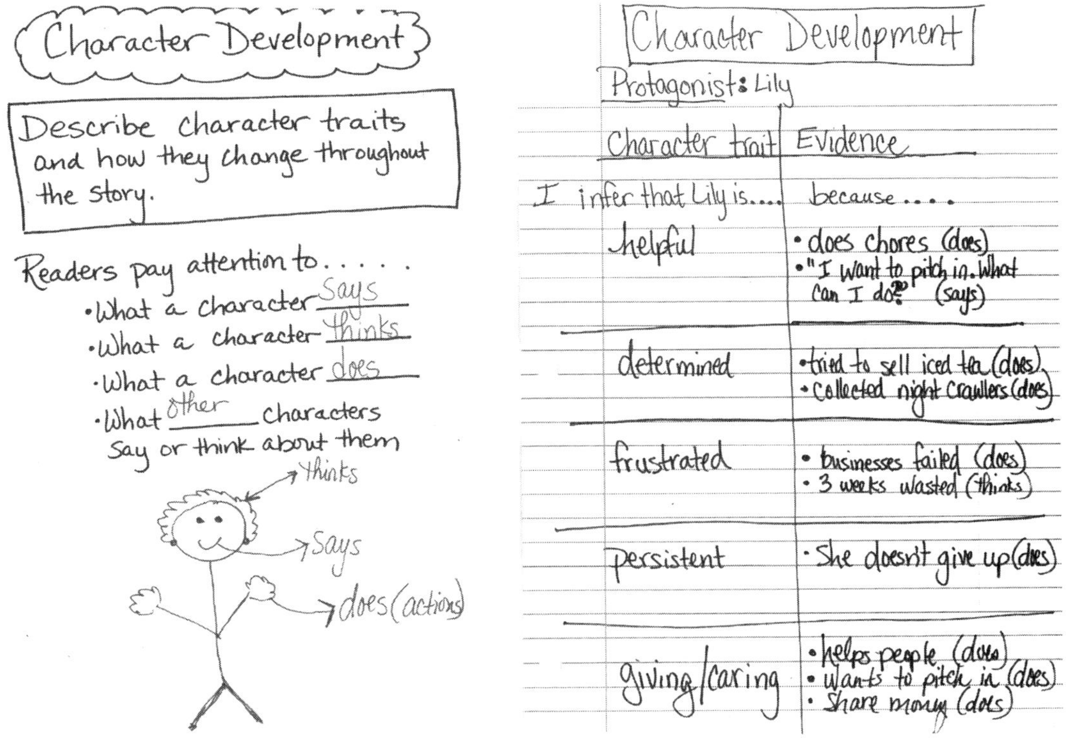

The work you share with students in your notebook will show them what a response to reading looks like and becomes a key resource and reminder for the writing you ask them to complete in readers' notebooks.

READERS' NOTEBOOKS BOOST COMPREHENSION

The research of Graham, Harris, and Santangelo (2015) shows that when students write about books they can read, their comprehension of the book can improve by 24 percentage points. That's why writing about reading is part of our guided practice lessons and should be part of interactive read-alouds and instructional reading as well.

I recommend that readers' notebooks remain at school and that students use marble covered composition notebooks instead of spiral bound notebooks. Marble covered composition notebooks encourage students to keep every jot, picture, phrase, and question because if they tear out pages, the notebook falls apart. Moreover, by saving all pages, students can skim and review work, self-evaluate, consider their progress, and set reasonable goals.

Many of the developing readers I learn with arrive in fifth grade unable to write a complete sentence. For them, notebook writing is a huge challenge, so it's best to have them start by writing lists and phrases, allowing them to develop thinking and writing fluency. At first, students' notebook writing will be literal—often a list of facts or jots about what happened in their books. The modeling and thinking aloud you do as you cold write responses in your notebooks enable students to infer, compare and contrast, explain cause and effect, identify problems and solutions, draw conclusions, note themes and main ideas, apply literary elements, make predictions, and ask questions. By mid-school year, most students are responding to reading in ways that mirror the high-level thinking in interactive read-alouds and your modeled writing in notebooks. The three notebook entries for the same fifth grade student shown in Figure 2.6 illustrate the progress in writing about reading that many made during the year.

Writing in notebooks encourages students to think on paper, and the partner discussion lessons support their writing practice by offering opportunities to write about reading. However, it's important that you listen to students' questions and comments and watch their behavior as asking students to complete more and more work can result in developing learners experiencing cognitive overload.

FIGURE 2.5: STACEY YOST'S NOTEBOOK FOR THE FIRST CHUNK OF TEXT FROM JACK AND THE BEANSTALK RETOLD BY STEVEN KELLOGG ILLUSTRATES HOW SHE JOTS NOTES AND THINKS THROUGH CAUSE/EFFECT.

FIGURE 2.6: AS TEACHERS THINK ALOUD AND COLD WRITE, STUDENTS BEGIN TO UNDERSTAND HOW TO THINK DEEPLY ON PAPER. NOTE BRANDON'S PROGRESS FROM AUGUST TO JANUARY TO APRIL!

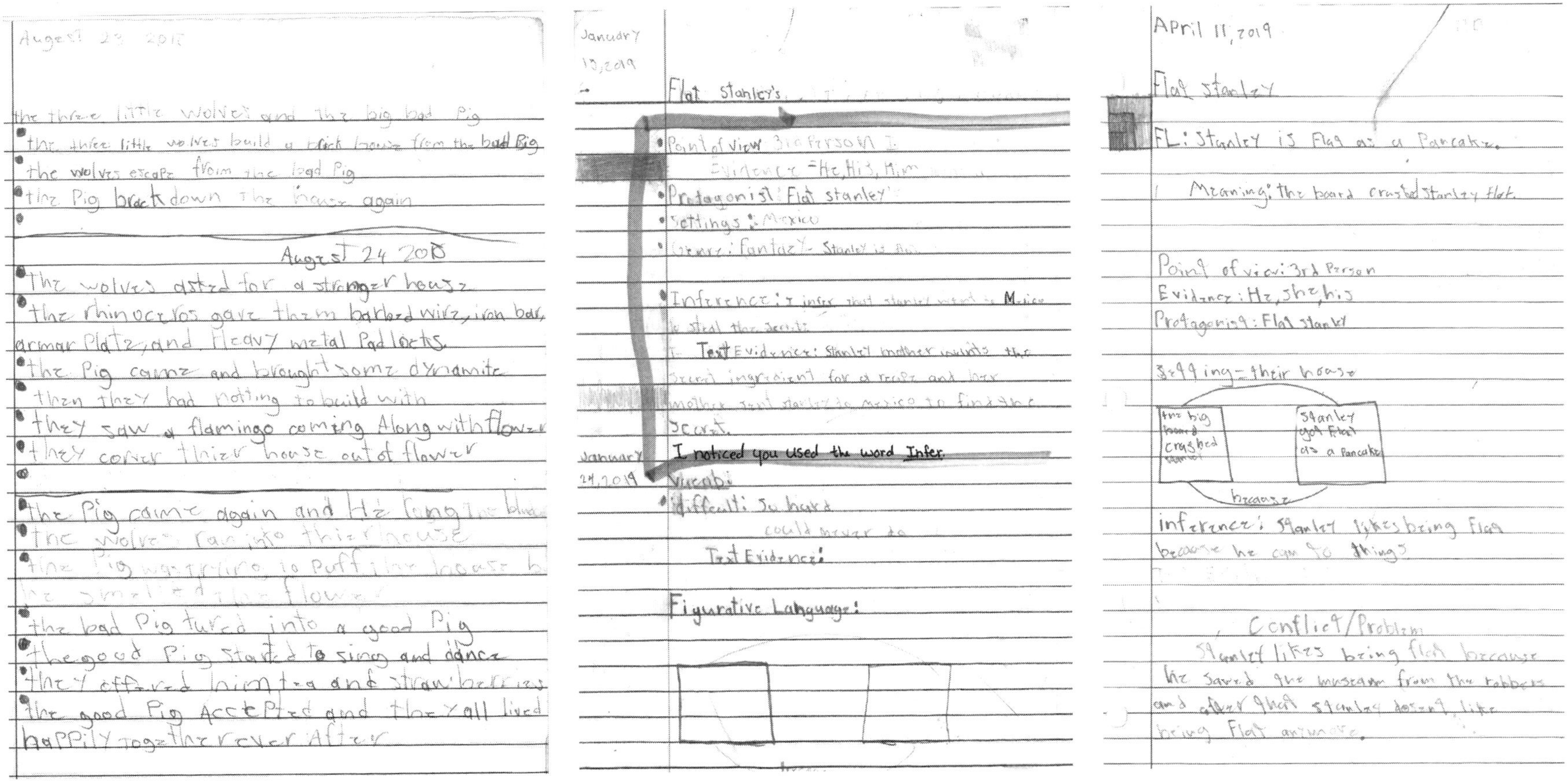

AVOID COGNITIVE OVERLOAD

When you have a strong desire and commitment to move developing readers forward as quickly as possible, you should pause and reflect on cognitive overload. When input for students exceeds the background knowledge they have or when students try to complete two things at the same time, such as watching a video and skimming a text or looking at photographs and thinking about the figurative language the author used to describe each one, they can stop processing information because they are on cognitive overload (Meacham, 2017). In other words, too much too fast can backfire!

Developing readers are susceptible to cognitive overload because they lack the experiences, prior knowledge, vocabulary, and tools to unpack a text's meaning. To avoid cognitive overload, the guided practice lessons in this book focus on vocabulary and one or two strategies at a time. Some lessons will also include visualization because developing readers benefit from extra practice picturing information. Being able to visualize is a sign of understanding information. Know what you want students to learn and design lessons that support your purpose.

Here are some tips to consider:

- Use anchor charts and support the reader's understanding of the lesson.
- Break up complex work into small doable tasks.
- Keep the learner focused on the lesson and avoid bringing in information and visuals that make it difficult for the student to maintain his/her focus.
- Develop opportunities for students to pair-share, reflect, and share what they understand.
- Encourage students to ask questions.

Watch, listen, and read your students' body language during a lesson. If they appear confused, simplify, slow down, and refocus the lesson on one objective or skill.

TIME TO REFLECT

Use the questions to have in-the-head conversations with yourself and/or with a colleague who is reading this book.

- How do daily teacher read-alouds and independent reading support developing readers?
- How do you plan to enlarge the vocabulary of developing readers? Why is this important?
- How do teachers' notebooks support learners?
- What are some ways to avoid cognitive overload in shared reading lessons?

PART 2

Teaching the Guided Practice Lessons

The lessons in this section offer choices—for you and your students. You know your students' needs and you know the strategies they should practice. That's why it's *you* who chooses lessons to nudge your students' reading progress forward. There's no special order to the lessons; it's your students who define the order. As they make progress with reading, enlarging their vocabulary, and thinking about texts, you'll select lessons that will continue to support their growth as readers. Before we dive into the lessons, though, let's look at the types and components of guided practice lessons, as well as how they support students and help reading growth.

TWO TYPES OF GUIDED PRACTICE LESSONS: PARTNER DISCUSSION AND SHARED READING

Both lessons have a common purpose: to enlarge students' vocabulary and background knowledge and to provide practice with using details to think deeply about each text. To achieve this purpose, students will work on two different kinds of lessons.

Partner discussion lessons require you to do more explicit teaching by modeling how to write notebook responses and use context to determine the meaning of words. Students pair up to complete word work, discuss questions, and respond to prompts in their notebooks. These lessons offer students much needed practice in completing authentic reading tasks that are part of instructional reading and rely more heavily on students

Writing about reading in notebooks can improve students' comprehension.

learning to write responses in their notebooks, working together, and scaffolding tasks for each other.

Shared reading lessons invite students to solve reading challenges independently. These lessons require that you preplan, select texts ideal for problem solving, build students' background knowledge, and pose questions, but then allow students space. The goal of shared reading is for students to do the work and practice reading and thinking about texts independently. Gaining independence along with enlarging vocabulary and background knowledge enables them to enjoy independent reading and choose to read more at school and home. Some texts are more difficult, and with those, I invite students to pair up and support one another.

For each guided practice lesson, you'll find estimates of the amount of time you'll need for each day you and students collaborate on lessons. It's okay if you need extra time as students learn

and absorb new information at different rates. The graphic in Figure 3.1 shows side-by-side outlines followed by detailed descriptions of what each type of lesson contains to make the structure of these lessons clear. Appendixes F and G offer guidelines for planning your own shared reading and partner discussions lessons, and Appendixes H and J provide suggested resources for short prose texts and poetry books.

FIGURE 3.1: A COMPARISON OF THE PURPOSE OF THE TWO TYPES OF GUIDED PRACTICE LESSONS

Partner Discussion Lessons	Shared Reading Lessons
Purpose of the lesson	Purpose of the lesson
Lesson materials	Lesson materials
Part 1. Teacher prepares students to read; students working together. • Reading the poem • Focus on word building • Model cold writing in your teacher's notebook	Part 1. Pre-teach • Build background knowledge • Introduce new vocabulary
Part 2. Partner work • Prompts for paired discussion • Notebook writing	Part 2. Start the shared reading lesson • Divide text into meaningful chunks • Ask questions to stir students' thinking • Wrap up
Part 3. Teacher assesses • Reflect and intervene	Part 3. Teacher assesses • Students complete the anchor chart • Clarify thinking and extend ideas • Reflect and intervene

THE STRUCTURE OF PARTNER DISCUSSION LESSONS USING POETRY AND SHORT TEXTS

For these partner discussion lessons, pair up students who are no more than a year apart in instructional reading levels, so they can learn from and support one another.

There are three parts to these lessons. In Part 1, the teacher prepares students to read the selection, models using context clues to determine the meaning of unfamiliar words,

as well as the strategy partners will practice. During this time, pairs try what's been modeled and support one another. This part closes asking teachers to model how to write a response in their notebooks so students understand expectations. Tips for completing the modeled writing will be in each lesson.

In Part 2, partners discuss the piece, supply text evidence to support their thinking, and complete notebook writing using your cold writing model as a resource. Pairs always have choices, for choice empowers them as thinkers and writers. Frequent partner discussions offer opportunities for each student to think about a response and clarify ideas so partners understand each other's reasoning and point of view. The discussion and writing prompts can be posted onto a whiteboard using your computer or a document camera.

Assessment and intervention guidelines are the focus of Part III. It's important for teachers to review students' written work and their notes on partner discussions to decide who can move on and who requires scaffolding or re-teaching.

THE STRUCTURE OF SHARED READING LESSONS

Teachers usually associate the phrase *shared reading* with big books teachers in grades K–2 read to model strategies as children sit on a rug close to their teacher. However, in their book, *Who's Doing the Work?* Jan Burkins and Kim Yaris point out that shared reading benefits students in intermediate grades *and* middle school (2018). I wholeheartedly agree with the authors, and the shared reading I've done with sixth graders showed me the benefits of this kind of guided practice.

Each shared reading lesson will spotlight the materials you and students need and preplanning notes that emerge from thinking deeply about the text and the lesson's focus. Students will work independently during shared reading lessons. With students, set shared reading expectations such as raise your hand and avoid interrupting a classmate.

In Part 1 of the shared reading lesson you'll build students' background knowledge of the text's topic, introduce challenging vocabulary, and have students use context to figure out meanings, as well as expand their vocabulary by featuring sets of related words.

The shared reading lessons also ask you to set up an *anchor chart* to record students' responses to a text. At the end of the lesson under "Teacher Assesses," students reread the notes on the chart and add ideas as well as make adjustments. Write adjustments and additions using a different colored marker so you can see, at a glance, students' suggestions. Having a chart with a record of students' thinking enables

FIGURE 3.2: ANCHOR FOR "JANE GOODALL: A PORTRAIT OF DETERMINATION"—A * NEXT TO STUDENTS' RESPONSES INDICATES IDEAS ADDED DURING PART 3 OF THE LESSONS.

you to assess their progress and decide on your next instructional moves. Moreover, the chart shows students how to organize their thinking and also becomes a model for students' notebook writing about other texts they read for instruction. Figure 3.2 shows an example.

In Part 2, you'll start the shared reading lesson, divide the text into meaningful and manageable chunks followed by suggested questions. Avoid the temptation of filling silence with an answer. Give students think time. Ask another question, to stir or redirect their thinking. Always take time to wrap up the lesson by noticing what worked well. Doing this shows students the kind of responses and thinking they did that worked and also reveals their progress with analyzing and thinking deeply about a text. This is the type of guided practice developing readers need to reach deeper levels of comprehension, enlarge vocabulary, improve fluency, and ultimately gain confidence and skill as independent readers.

Part 3 closes the lesson by taking about 15 to 20 minutes to adjust, refine, and add details to anchor chart notes with students' help. Invite students to whisper-read, read silently, or choral read the text, then reread the notes on the anchor chart and suggest revisions and/or add extra evidence to a response. Revisiting notes on the chart to clarify and extend ideas helps students experience that thinking about text is a process, not a one-shot deal. It also sends the message that deep thinking deserves time. Developing readers need the gift of time to process, think, share, and reflect on texts to prevent cognitive overload (see page 28). Once students develop a mental model of the noticing process, turn it over to them. The goal is for students to not only do the work but to also know what they did well. By using the gradual release model, students do the noticing. Such self-evaluation shows students their growth and in turn motivates them to read more and have the confidence to apply what they understand to their independent reading.

GUIDED PRACTICE AND THE GRADUAL RELEASE OF RESPONSIBILITY

The gradual release of responsibility model asks you to think aloud and model for students, and then have them practice with you close to them to support and answer questions. When they're ready, you can move students to independence with a task and point out what they are doing that shows you they're ready to work on their own. Pearson and Gallagher described this model in 1983; the model aligns with Lev Vygotsky's zones of proximal development (1978). At first, you do most of the work because students are in their learning zone and need scaffolds such as think-alouds and modeling. As students interact with you, ask questions, and practice applying a strategy to a text, they gain the proficiency and confidence that moves them from needing support to completing a task independently.

The guided practice lessons in this book include the gradual release of responsibility model (Fisher & Frey, 2013; Pearson & Gallagher, 1983). Both shared reading and partner discussion lessons open with you scaffolding the building of students' background knowledge and vocabulary prior to reading. Then, you turn the responsibility for discussing them over to students. You scaffold the reading of each text by first reading it aloud and having students follow silently. Sometimes, students choral read or share the reading with a partner. Responsibility for reading the text moves to students when they gather evidence to support discussions and complete notebook writing.

As students improve, teachers can decide whether to decrease the number of guided practice lessons and replace them with more instructional reading since guided practice is part of instructional reading (see pages 9–11). Extra time can also be used for students to write about reading in their notebooks, complete vocabulary work, confer with you, or read independently.

It's possible that students have absorbed a strategy using short texts, but when confronted with a longer text, they have difficulty applying it. I suggest using the guidelines in Appendix F to develop a guided practice lesson using a chapter from a book, a short story, article, or an excerpt from an informational text. Plan lessons with one or more team members because sharing the work includes feedback from colleagues and quickens the process.

FOUR TEACHING TIPS FOR GUIDED PRACTICE LESSONS

The tips that follow emerged from questions teachers frequently ask.

1. **Whole class or small group?** Decide whether you'll present the lesson to your entire class or to a small group. If you're working with a small group, invite students not working with you to read independently or complete notebook work.

2. **Why silent reading?** When you read a text aloud, ask students to follow silently. The goal of guided practice and independent reading is to develop students' in-the-head silent reading voices. In addition, you might have to ask some students to reread a passage silently to improve recall of details as rereading is an excellent fix-up strategy.

3. **When should students read out loud?** If you need to hear students read to assess their fluency and decoding, do that separately with a short section of a prose text or a poem. Because poems are meant to be heard, you can ask your developing readers to read them out loud to practice expressive, fluent reading. Help students who are dependent on reading out loud to understand that doing this slows the reading process down and puts them at a disadvantage as they move from intermediate to middle and high school where reading demands increase. You will need to listen to some students read aloud, but I recommend that you then have them read the selection silently and explain why.

4. **How to wrap up the lessons?** Notice what students did that worked without naming individuals and explain why it worked. For example, I might say this about inferring: "I noticed that all of you used a person's decisions to infer and you supported your inferences by paraphrasing a specific decision."

HOW CAN GUIDED PRACTICE LESSONS LEAD TO READING GROWTH?

Features in the lessons support progress in reading. Each lesson builds students' background knowledge by having them view and listen to one or two videos. A great equalizer, video allows developing middle grade and middle school readers to easily access information. This part of the lesson is key to students' success because prior knowledge, including enlarging vocabulary, can make texts readable and enjoyable. Finally, students have to use text details to infer, visualize, draw conclusions, identify personality traits, find themes, and so forth because depth of thinking is what develops a desire to read and motivates learners to read independently. This motivation to select and read books can develop from guided practice as students improve fluency, decoding, enlarge their vocabulary and background knowledge, and experience meaningful discussions and notebook writing. The better readers students become, the more likely they are to read independently for pleasure at school and at home! Help your students grow as readers by choosing the lessons they need to move forward.

HOW ARE THE LESSONS IN THIS BOOK ORGANIZED?

You'll find a total of 24 lessons in Part II. Chapter 3 contains 12 Partner Discussion Lessons, and Chapter 4 contains 12 Shared Reading lessons. Every group of lessons centers on particular skills or strategies, such as figurative language and imagery, inferring and visualizing, and so on. You'll find the corresponding poem or short text directly before the lesson. ***Remember, the order of lessons is your choice and depends on the needs of your students.***

To help you select a lesson that's ideal for the readers you teach, on page 30 you'll find a chart that organizes lessons by specific reading strategies. Note that every lesson prepares students to read by building background knowledge and enlarging vocabulary. You'll also find in Appendixes F and G guidelines for planning your own shared reading and partner discussion lessons, as well as two additional poems and two short texts by David Harrison that you can use in Appendix I. In addition, Appendix H provides a list of resources for short texts and Appendix J offers suggestions for poetry books to explore for designing your own guided practice lessons.

HOW MANY LESSONS SHOULD STUDENTS COMPLETE?

That question is the elephant in the room. I can't recommend a definite number because I don't know your students' strengths, needs, and background knowledge. However, I suggest you start by setting aside two consecutive weeks in a month to plan and present the lessons and then make adjustments based on what your students can do and what they need more practice with (see sample schedules on pages 122 and 123). Reduce or add lessons each month if your assessments show students require less or more practice. Lessons include *about* time frames, and these will also vary. Follow your students' lead and adjust the time it takes for them to complete a lesson throughout the year; time suggestions are only estimates.

Remember, guided practice will be your instructional reading. However, the guided practice lessons in this book are not an entire reading curriculum. They are the part of your curriculum that can help you decide next instructional moves. Research clearly shows that for students to improve their reading skill, reading more books and reading longer books make a difference (Brozo, Shiel, & Topping, 2008).

HOW DO I KNOW WHEN TO INTERVENE?

Each lesson closes by inviting you to review students' reactions to the lesson, your observational notes, students' notebook writing, and any other interactions. If most or all of a group of students *don't get* a lesson, take a deep breath and try to discover why. Avoid blaming the students, the lesson, or yourself. The best strategy is to ask students, "Can you help me understand why you weren't able to complete your notebook writing or discuss the piece with your partner?" At first, you may get no response. Keep asking because once you've established trusting relationships with students, they will risk sharing lesson roadblocks with you. The query may start to resonate with

them if you also explain that their feedback can help you adjust the lesson so it benefits their learning. In addition, here are questions to reflect on and connect to students' responses (or their lack of responding):

- Did students have enough background knowledge to understand the text?
- Would more than one to two readings have boosted recall and comprehension?
- Did the topic resonate with students?
- Would it be best to start with a video and tap into students' visual learning ability to enlarge their background knowledge?
- Are there words and/or concepts that students found challenging? Should these have been discussed prior to the lesson?
- Do students require more modeling and scaffolding to figure out the meaning of words using context clues?

WHY SHOULD STUDENTS SELF-EVALUATE?

After students complete two to three lessons, invite them to reflect on a skill or strategy they practiced (see Appendix D). These short self-evaluations can also help you decide whether to intervene, have a student practice with a peer, or move on to a new lesson that offers additional practice with the same strategy. When students can talk about their learning and progress while conferring with you as well as write about what they understand, they eventually develop the metacognition that can help them identify what they know and when they require additional practice. The self-evaluations by fifth graders Jay and Addison in Figures 3.3 and 3.4 illustrate how reflective thinking and writing benefit you and students.

HOW DO I CHOOSE TEXTS?

Developing readers in Grades 4 and up have a limited reading vocabulary and background knowledge because most of them do little or

FIGURE 3.3: ADDISON CAN EXPLAIN HOW HE FIGURED OUT THE MEANING OF *SHACKLES*.

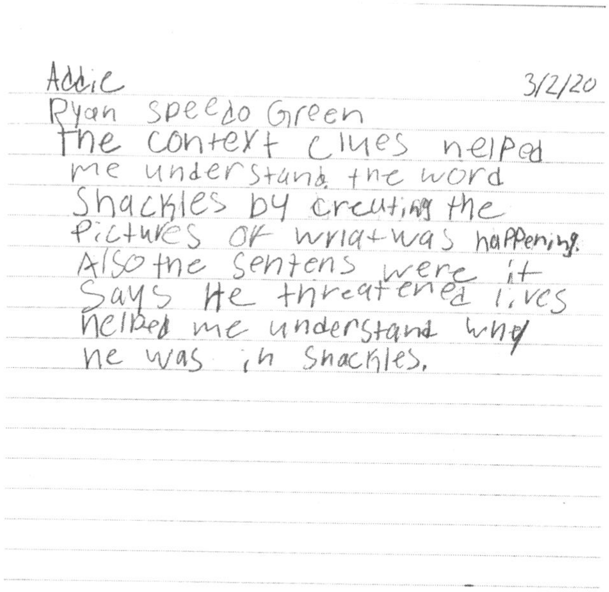

Addie   3/2/20
Ryan speedo Green
The context clues helped
me understand the word
Shackles by creating the
Pictures of what was happening.
Also the sentens were it
says He threatened lives
helped me understand why
he was in shackles.

FIGURE 3.4: JAY POINTS OUT HOW THE VIDEO GAVE HIM THE BACKGROUND KNOWLEDGE TO PICTURE THE RAIN FOREST.

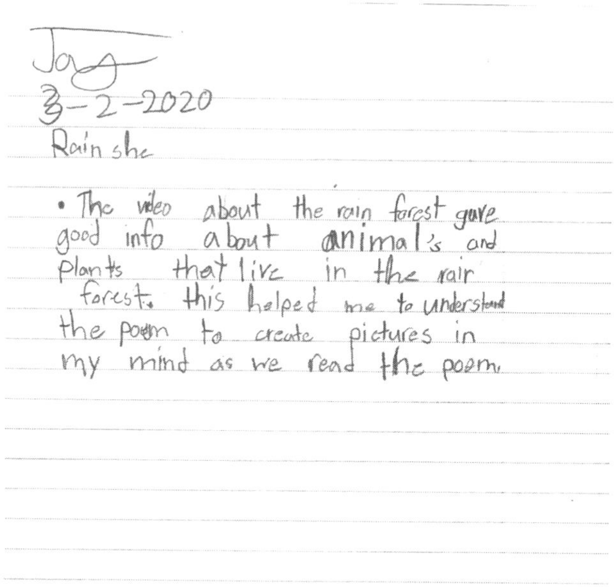

Jay
3-2-2020
Rain she

• The video about the rain forest gave
good info about animal's and
Plants that live in the rain
forest. this helped me to understand
the poem to create pictures in
my mind as we read the poem.

no reading at school and at home. Even if they watch television, their background knowledge depends on the programs they watch, and these don't necessarily build the prior knowledge required to comprehend texts across the curriculum. Discussions with middle grade and middle school teachers who work with developing readers revealed a need for students to read a variety of genres as well as learn about diverse cultures, history, geography, science, and people who overcame obstacles and changed the world. David Harrison has written original texts and poems for the lessons in this book, and the guidelines in Appendix F and G can help you as you move into planning your own lessons around texts.

The lessons in this book are built around poems and short texts that stretch students' thinking and application of strategies. These texts might challenge or even frustrate students if read independently. However, a primary goal of guided practice is to provide students support from their teacher and/or a peer partner to improve fluency and expression, vocabulary, recall and comprehension, and the quality of discussions. When you are ready to plan your own lessons, you'll want to look for texts that are somewhat challenging but not frustrating to your readers. Appendixes H and J provide recommended sources for texts and poems.

HOW DO I INTRODUCE TEXTS SO STUDENTS WANT TO READ THEM?

The lessons ask students to read short narrative and informational texts as well as poetry. Before plunging students into lessons that use poems, help them enjoy the poem's language, images, and content. Then, instead of asking students to analyze a poem and answer questions, reserve time for them to hear, say, and enjoy the poem. Let students live through the poem, have what Louise Rosenblatt (1978) calls an aesthetic response, interactions between reader and poet that can stir emotions and bond readers to the text.

- **Poetry.** First, read the poem out loud and have students follow by reading it silently. You're modeling fluency, expressive reading, and how punctuation signals pauses. Then, organize students into partners and invite them to read the poem to one another. Circulate and pause to listen to students read, celebrate their expression, and support those who ask questions or need your help. Each group of lesson choices in Part II of this book will have two poems.

After students have completed the lessons, invite them to choose a poem, practice reading it every day to their partner, then volunteer to perform it to the class. Research on the relationship between practice and performance reveals progress in students' fluency, vocabulary development, and comprehension (Rasinski & Griffith, 2011). (See pages 117–121 in the concluding chapter for organizing practice and performance of poems.) Adding this to class routines for developing readers has the potential to build self-confidence but also improve reading skill. Once students have enjoyed the language, meaning, and emotional responses to a poem, it's time to introduce the guided practice lesson.

- **Short Prose Texts.** Prose selections ask developing readers to read more and use context clues to figure out the meaning of challenging words. Longer texts can increase students' ability to remember and recall information introduced at the beginning of the text and use it in the middle or near the end. These texts build students' background knowledge of narratives, biography, memoir, and informational texts.

I suggest that you also read aloud the short prose selections. Just hearing and enjoying a text before starting the formal lesson creates a familiarity with the content. This extra reading can increase students' prior knowledge and support their approaching the lesson with an "I can do this" mindset.

WHAT MATERIALS DO I NEED FOR LESSONS TO RUN SMOOTHLY AND SUCCESSFULLY?

It's helpful to know up front the tools and materials you and students will need so that each guided practice lesson moves forward like a well-oiled bicycle.

- **A document camera** to point out details and vocabulary in the text and to model cold notebook writing

- **A laptop or iPad** for projecting videos onto a whiteboard

- **Reader's notebooks** for every student to write about his/her reading. When taking notes or writing a new entry, have students write their name, date, and the title of the poem or short text. Dating and heading entries makes it easier for students to find a specific one.

- **A teacher's notebook** for yourself, so you can model notebook writing for students

- **Student folders** for storing guided practice texts, a 4 × 6 index card, and a blank piece of paper

- **A plastic crate** to hold students' folders for each section you teach

- **A clipboard and sticky notes** to jot what you observed about a student as you circulate to watch, answer questions, and offer support

- **Group or whole class lesson?** Decide before starting so you can engage students not participating in meaningful reading or writing about reading

- **Seating arrangements** that allow for side-by-side partner work

- **Copies of texts** for each student participating in the guided practice lesson

- **Copies of the self-evaluation form** (see Appendix D) to give to students when you want them to reflect on a lesson

REMINDERS FOR THE GUIDED PRACTICE LESSONS

Revisit these reminders frequently to support students as they complete guided practice lessons. If students struggle with any aspect of a lesson, scaffold the learning by thinking aloud and modeling.

- Keep students' file folders with poems, short text, index card, and blank sheet of paper in plastic crates. Each section you teach has its own crate. Or you can store these in separate cubbies or different places on a bookshelf.

- Use the index card or sheet of paper to cover up parts of a poem or text you're not reading.

- Whenever you circulate among students to watch and support, carry a clipboard with sticky notes. Jot important noticings on a dated sticky note that also has the students' name.

- Lead a quick review of key points of the previous day's lesson.

- Have students rewatch videos if they need more viewing time to process information.

- Have partners collaborate for an entire lesson. How often pairs learn together is your call.

- Make sure you remind students to jot notes before completing a notebook entry.

- Ask students to complete the self-evaluation form once they've completed two paired discussion lessons.

MAKE SURE YOU READ THE FINAL CHAPTER

At the end of the groups of guided practice lessons is a closing chapter titled *Next Steps for Guided Practice and Growth in Reading*. In this chapter, you'll explore guidelines for using the poems and short texts to increase students' fluency and expressive reading, as well as some teaching and learning reminders to guide you as you continue to integrate guided practice lessons in instructional reading.

The online companion includes suggestions for moving guided practice lessons online in a distance learning setting, too.

CHAPTER 3

Partner Discussion Lessons

Jennifer Harrison's fourth graders read "What Was She Thinking?"—a poem for two voices about Jane Goodall.

Students experience meaningful literary conversations by discussing the poems and short texts with a partner. Discussion improves recall as well as answering open-ended questions— queries that have more than one answer. These lessons also provide opportunities for students to use details to make inferences, draw conclusions, visualize, and connect ideas. In addition, teachers will develop a writing-about-reading model in their notebooks that students can use as a resource when they write about the poem or short text.

To access the suggested video to build background knowledge for poems or short, prose texts, use the QR code next to the lesson or simply enter the title of the video into your preferred search engine.

Jane Goodall
Gombe National Park
Lake Tanganyika, Africa
1960

What Was She Thinking?

1st voice
What was she thinking,

going to live with chimps?

searching to catch a glimpse,

Living among them,
day after day,
doing whatever she must,

as she wrote and reported
back to the world

The chimps taught Jane,

Science has learned
so much from Jane,

2nd voice

camped in a jungle,

What was she thinking,
girl in her twenties,

then working a year,
and working another
learning to earn their trust?

decades passed
for Jane and her chimps
near the Tanganyika shore

like no one had before.

and Jane taught us
the amazing lives of chimps.

and it all began with a glimpse.

Lesson 1

PARTNER DISCUSSIONS USING THE POEM FOR TWO VOICES, "WHAT WAS SHE THINKING?"

Purpose: To have students use their recall of details to reflect on what causes people to make decisions that affect the path of their lives. Students read this poem for two voices with their partner—each reading one of the voices.

Day 1: About 20 minutes

Part 1. Teacher Prepares Students to Read

- Organize students in partners.

- With students, watch the short video, "First Look at Jane/National Geographic" (2:51).

https://youtu.be/rcL4jnGTL1U

- Have students turn-and-talk and discuss what they learned about Jane and chimpanzees from the video, asking, *Why do you think a photographer was sent to photograph what Jane had seen?* Invite volunteers to share what they learned.

- Ask students to jot what they recall in their notebooks.

- Circulate to observe, listen, support, and take notes.

Reading the Poem

- Give students a copy of the poem and their file folders for storing the poem.

- Read the poem out loud as students follow silently.

- Ask partners to choose which voice they'll read. Have students read their voice with their partner.

Day 2: About 15–20 minutes

Focus on Word Building

- Reread both voices and stop after "searching to catch a glimpse." Think aloud and explain that Jane's situation—watching chimps in the jungle—helped you understand that "catching a glimpse" means a quick look. Invite students to ask questions.

- Ask students to choral read with you beginning with the words "decades passed" and ending with "Back to the world." Ask, *What do you think is passing and what clues helped you figure that out?* Next, ask if anyone knows what a decade is? If not, introduce the Latin root *deca*, meaning 10, and see if they can figure out the meaning of *decade* and *decades*.

Model Cold Writing in Your Teacher's Notebook

- Use this prompt to jot notes and cold write in front of students: *Connect the video you watched to Jane's decision to stay at Gombe.* (Notes: chimps made and used tools to eat termites; wants to learn what else chimps can do)

- Cold write in front of students turning notes into sentences.

Day 3: 20–30 minutes

Part 2. Partner Work: Recall and Evaluate Decisions

Pairs discuss recall questions. Then choose two open-ended questions to discuss. Ask students to offer details in the poem they used to answer questions.

Prompts for Paired Discussions

- What did Jane do in the jungle? (recall)

- How did Jane teach the world what she learned? (recall)

- What does Jane's decision to stay in the jungle show about her personality?

- Why does the poet close the poem with "and it all began with a glimpse?"

- Why do you think Jane studied chimps for decades?

Notebook Writing

Take a few minutes to review the cold writing you modeled for students. Remind them to head a page in their notebook with name, date, and the title of the poem.

- Draw an illustration for this poem and write a caption.

- Ask students to select two prompts they discussed. For each one, have them jot a few notes and use the notes to write complete sentences.

- Watch another video about Jane Goodall on YouTube. Then, write a list of all you recalled and learned. Jot notes and turn these into sentences.

- Circulate among students to support, observe, and jot notes.

Day 4: 15–20 minutes

Part 3. Teacher Assesses

- Use your observations and notes along with students' notebook writing.

- Talk to students when you need to clarify your thoughts.

Reflect and Intervene

- On sticky notes, jot what students did well and areas they need support, and then store these in your loose-leaf notebook.

- Scaffold notebook writing using this poem by supporting students as they turn notes into sentences.

- Help students set a goal for the next guided practice and jot it in their notebook.

Jorge Muñoz: An American Hero

[1]Jorge Muñoz was born in 1964 in Colombia, South America. When he was nine, his father was killed by a flying rock from a passing truck. His mother, Doris, did her best to care for her son and daughter but times were hard. After ten years, she finally made her way into the country without acceptable documentation. Without the legal papers, she had to be very careful in order to remain in the United States and go to New York to find better work. There she became a live-in nanny. When she had saved enough money, she sent for Jorge and his sister Luz, who also came as illegal immigrants.

[2]Doris and her children made new lives in New York. By the time Jorge was 23, he, his mother, and his sister had all become American citizens. Luz went to work for the Social Security Administration. Jorge found work as a school bus driver. Their incomes helped when Doris developed painful arthritis and had to retire.

[3]Then something happened the year Jorge was 40 that would change his life and the lives of others. He saw hunger in the eyes and faces of a group of men gathered near the corner of Roosevelt Avenue and 73rd Street in Jackson Heights, Queens. When he stopped to talk, he learned they were looking for work, any kind of work. Some were homeless and slept nights under a nearby bridge. Jorge figured that many of these men were undocumented immigrants as he had once been. When he learned that some restaurants threw away leftover food, he formed a plan.

[4]One evening after work, Jorge put food into paper sacks and took them to the hungry men. They were amazed. Jorge began taking them something to eat three nights a week. As the line of grateful men grew, cold snacks became hot meals. As more and more men counted on Jorge for one good meal each night, he was soon providing food seven nights a week. His mother began helping him cook in their tiny kitchen. His sister helped. Friends pitched in. Jorge climbed out of bed early to plan his day before he went to work so he would be ready to deliver meals each night at 9:30. By 2010, Jorge guessed he had served 70,000 meals. To serve even more hungry people, Jorge Muñoz created a foundation to raise money for more food.

[5]As word spread about the quiet hero in Queens, New York, his story attracted so much attention that he was presented with the Presidential Citizen's Medal, the second-highest civilian honor in the land. President Obama said, "These honorees' lives stand as shining examples of what it means to be an American." Jorge's mother tells of a day when he was seven and a hungry man came by their house. They had no food to spare so Jorge gave the man his plate and ate bread for his own meal.

The poet William Wordsworth wrote, "The child is father of the man." In Jorge's case, both the child and the man are heroes.

Lesson 2

PARTNER DISCUSSIONS OF THE SHORT TEXT, "JORGE MUÑOZ: AN AMERICAN HERO"

Purpose: To practice making connections and drawing conclusions. "Jorge Muñoz: An American Hero" is a story that will reach deeply into students' hearts causing them to react emotionally to his story. The deep, emotional connections students make to Jorge will enable them to draw conclusions about Munoz, his actions, decisions, and honors bestowed on him.

Day 1: About 20–30 minutes

Part 1. Teacher Prepares Students to Read

- Organize students into partners.

- Have pairs discuss, *What makes a person a hero?* When partners share their ideas, record them on chart paper. If students have difficulty with this, start them with: courage, stands up for what's right, and then ask for their ideas.

- Ask students to head a notebook page and jot a list of what they remembered from their discussion. Invite students to share one idea from their list as a review.

- Circulate to observe, listen, and take notes to determine how much students remembered.

- Give each student a copy of the text and their file folders, and have them retrieve the blank sheet of paper.

Reading the Text

- Read one paragraph at a time out loud with expression. Students follow silently.

- Stop after the second paragraph, share the emotions you're feeling and explain why.

- Ask pairs to discuss what they know about being an *illegal immigrant*. Have them share with class.

- Stop after the third and fourth paragraphs and ask pairs to turn-and-talk and share the emotions they feel. Have students explain what in the text caused these feelings.

- Read to the end. Ask students to explain how President Obama concluded that Jorge showed what it means to be an American.

- Review the chart on qualities of a hero. Ask students to add ideas and adjust any on the chart.

Day 2: About 20 minutes

Focus on Word Building: Context Clues

Think aloud and model how you use context to figure out the meaning of *retire* in the last line of the second paragraph. Explain how "painful arthritis" helped you know that retire meant stopped working. Point out that her children earned money and that made it easier for Doris to stop working.

- Ask pairs to silently reread the fourth paragraph, and use context to explain *providing* and *pitched in*. Pairs share, discuss, and adjust their thinking if necessary.

- Explain the term *foundation*. Help students understand that Jorge started one to raise money without paying taxes so the dollars could go to feeding homeless and assisting them with finding work.

Model Cold Writing in Your Teacher's Notebook

- Use this question to show how you jot notes and then use the notes to write a few sentences: *Why did Jorge create a foundation to raise money?* (Notes: a foundation can accept donations; it's not for profit or making money; it's a charity. Jorge needed a charity to raise lots of money.)

- Cold write in front of students turning notes into sentences.

Day 3: About 20–25 minutes

Part 2. Students Work With a Partner

Prompts for Paired Discussions

Pairs choose three questions that ask them to use text details to draw conclusions. Encourage students to reread or skim parts to find evidence and paraphrase it in their words. Draw conclusions about:

- Why Jorge's life changed when he was 40

- Jorge's personality traits using what he did for others

- Why you think his family and friends pitched in

- Why Jorge received the Presidential Citizen's Medal

- Do you believe Jorge is a hero? Make sure you explain why a person is thought to be a hero.

- What does the poet Wordsworth mean by "The child is father of the man?"

Notebook Writing

Take a few minutes to review the cold writing you modeled for students. Remind them to head a page in their notebook with name, date, and the title of this selection.

- Head a page in your notebook with name, date, and the title of this selection.

- Choose a question you discussed with your partner, write it in your notebook, jot notes, and then put them into sentences.

- In paragraph three, use context clues to define *gathered* and *homeless*.

- Was Jorge a hero? Yes or No. Choose a position and jot notes that support it. Turn notes into a short paragraph with complete sentences.

- Circulate among students to support, observe, and jot notes.

Day 4: 15–20 minutes

Part 3. Teacher Assesses

- Read students' notebook entries on defining words using context clues and drawing conclusions. Make a list of students who need more practice.

Reflect and Intervene

- Decide whether you will scaffold or the student can make progress working with a peer.

- Re-teach the lesson using this text or you can choose a text from Appendix I.

- Once students have completed two to three lessons, ask them to complete part of the self-evaluation form (see Appendix D) and discuss it with them during a short conference. This will support your assessment data.

Escape Artist

[1]*Tighten the knot,*
double the tape,
a few minutes
behind the drape,
and the clever magician
would always escape.

[2]A boy was born in Hungary
in 1874, his name
was Erik Weisz.

[3]*From straight jacket*
as tight as skin,
with margin of error
razor thin,
he'd wriggle out,
bow and grin.

[4]Who knew, when Erik Weisz was four,
he would come to America?

[5]*Plunged in water*
inside a box,
he'd hold his breath,
pick the locks,
and stun the crowd,
that clever fox.

[6]Who knew, when Erik Weisz was nine,
he'd be a trapeze artist?

[7]*Hung by his heels*
from building cranes,
cast in prisons,
bound in chains,
no one could match
his wit and brains.

[8]And how could anybody know,
back in 1874, that Erik Weisz . . .

[9]*There was no lock*
he couldn't tame.
Far and wide
they knew his name.
Where he performed,
the people came.

[10]would gain world fame
as the one and only
Harry Houdini?

Lesson 3

PARTNER DISCUSSIONS USING THE POEM, "ESCAPE ARTIST"

Purpose: To introduce students to a poem within a poem; to use text details to visualize. The free verse poem poses questions to set up the rhymed poem in italics that chronicles the feats of the daring magician, Harry Houdini.

Day 1: About 20–30 minutes

Part 1. Teacher Prepares Students to Read

- Organize students into partners.

- Write Harry Houdini on a large chart and ask students: *What do you know about Houdini?* Record what they say on the chart.

- Watch the two videos that follow with students or choose others on YouTube.

- Short YouTube videos to watch: "Houdini Rope Escape" (1:13)

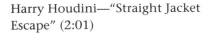

https://youtu.be/
EbvZZsYZmEY

Harry Houdini—"Straight Jacket Escape" (2:01)

https://youtu.be/
3r8qr-p9z5g

- Ask students to pair-share about how they felt after watching a video and explain what made them feel like that. Invite students to share with the class.

- Have students write their impressions of Houdini's feats in their notebooks. Circulate to support, listen, observe, and jot notes.

Reading the Poem

- Give students a copy of the poem and their file folders for storing texts.

- Read the poem out loud and ask students to follow silently.

- Divide the class in half and have one group choral read the italicized poem and the other group read the free verse poem.

Day 2: About 15–20 minutes

Focus on Word Building

- To help students visualize and understand what trapeze artists do, watch the very short and super-exciting YouTube video: "Flying Trapeze."

https://youtu.be/
Gi9ky8CBBzc

- Have students pair-share to discuss their reactions to the video. Then, ask them to discuss: *What qualities does a nine-year-old boy need to become a trapeze artist?* Students share their thoughts.

- Read the third stanza in italics and ask students what *plunged* means. Have them explain the clues that helped them figure out the meaning. Introduce *plunge*, *plunging*, and *plunger*, and discuss these related words.

- Write this sentence with *plunger* on the board and ask pairs to explain what a plunger does: Mom used the *plunger* to clear the clogged sink by pumping the rubber cup attached to the wooden stick up and down.

- Ask pairs to use *plunge* and *plunging* in a sentence and share their work.

- Ask students what they know about building cranes and if they've seen one?

- Find a photo of a construction crane, show to students and ask them to imagine how they would feel suspended upside-down from a crane. Invite students to share.

Model Cold Writing in Your Teacher's Notebook

- Show how you pull details from the first stanza to visualize and then describe what you see in your own words. (Notes: tighten knot, double tape, hide behind curtain (drape), escapes)

- Use the notes to cold write with words describing what you picture.

Part 2. Partner Work: Use Specific Details to Visualize and Find Personality Traits

Partners discuss details in the stanzas written in italics and help one another create a mental picture. Then, they use details to find personality traits.

Day 3: About 20–30 minutes

Prompts for Paired Discussions

- Reread the second stanza in italics. Select the details that help you visualize the scene and explain what you imagine.

- Repeat what you did using the second stanza in italics for stanzas three and four in italics.

- Explain what the simile "From a straight jacket/as tight as skin" helps you picture.

- What is the poet telling you about the "margin of error" by calling it "razor thin?"

- In the fourth stanza, why did Houdini's action "stun the crowd?"

- What does the poet hope you'll think by calling Houdini a "clever fox?"

- Why does the poet write, "Far and wide/ they knew his name" in the last stanza in italics?

- Reread the entire poem out loud with your partner. Identify three to four personality traits of Houdini and point out the details you used to identify each.

Notebook Writing

Take a few minutes to review the cold writing you modeled for students. Remind them to head a page in their notebook with name, date, and the title of the poem.

- Draw an illustration of one scene from the poem.

- Write a detailed description, in your own words, of one event in the poem.

- Fold a page in your notebook in half lengthwise. Write your heading and the title of the poem. On the right side jot "Personality Traits;" on the left side jot, "Text Evidence." List three personality traits for Houdini and note the details that helped you infer these traits.

- Circulate among students to support, observe, and jot notes.

Part 3. Teacher Assesses

- Use your observations and notes along with students' notebook writing.

- Talk to students when you need to clarify your thoughts.

Reflect and Intervene

- On sticky notes, jot what students did well and areas they need support, and then store these in your loose-leaf notebook to review and inform instructional moves.

- Scaffold notebook writing using this poem by supporting students as they turn notes into sentences.

- Help students set a goal for the next guided practice and jot it in their notebook.

FIGURE 3.5: WANDA WATERS MODELS MULTIPLE FORMS OF *PLUNGE* AND VISUALIZING. SHE POINTS OUT HOUDINI'S PERSONALITY TRAITS AND *COLD WRITES* TWO PARAGRAPHS.

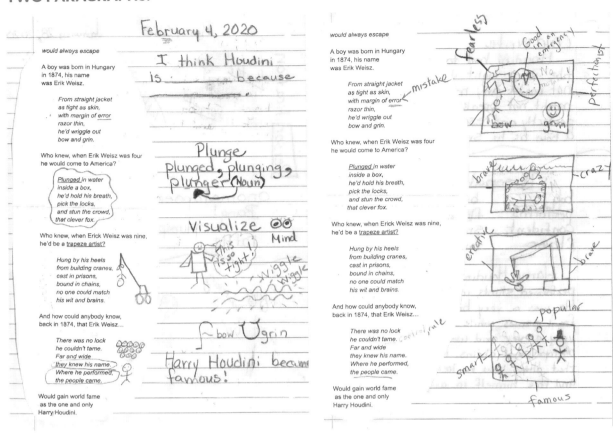

FIGURE 3.6: FIFTH GRADER, SHANE, ILLUSTRATES HOUDINI'S PERSONALITY TRAITS.

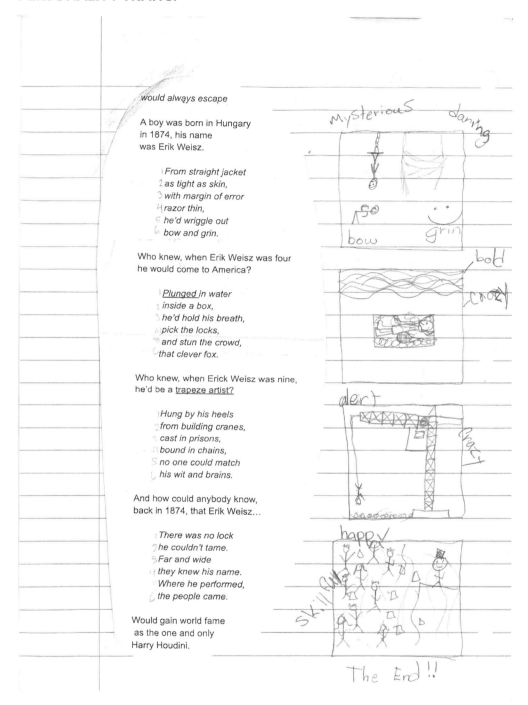

would always escape

A boy was born in Hungary in 1874, his name was Erik Weisz.

1 *From straight jacket*
2 *as tight as skin,*
3 *with margin of error*
4 *razor thin,*
5 *he'd wriggle out*
6 *bow and grin.*

Who knew, when Erik Weisz was four he would come to America?

1 *Plunged in water*
2 *inside a box,*
3 *he'd hold his breath,*
4 *pick the locks,*
5 *and stun the crowd,*
6 *that clever fox.*

Who knew, when Erick Weisz was nine, he'd be a trapeze artist?

1 *Hung by his heels*
2 *from building cranes,*
3 *cast in prisons,*
4 *bound in chains,*
5 *no one could match*
6 *his wit and brains.*

And how could anybody know, back in 1874, that Erik Weisz...

1 *There was no lock*
2 *he couldn't tame.*
3 *Far and wide*
4 *they knew his name.*
5 *Where he performed,*
6 *the people came.*

Would gain world fame as the one and only Harry Houdini.

What Was Early Humans' Greatest Invention?

[1]Nature has a way of inventing new species of living things. Today's humans—*Homo sapiens*—have been around about 200,000 years, but our story began long before that. Apes and people share a common <u>ancestor</u> who <u>roamed</u> around Africa between eight and six million years ago. Those first humans weren't like we are today, but they weren't apes either. Although they failed to last, other types came along. Scientists think as many as 15 or 20 kinds of humans lived at one time or another.

[2]We aren't related to those early types. They came and went on their own. But since everything started with that common ancestor, we might think of ourselves as distant cousins. Today, we humans rule the world, but back then, many other animals could run faster, bite harder, and send folks scrambling for their lives. It took a lot of improvements to take us from playing in trees to playing on cell phones.

[3]Here is my Top 10 list of improvements that made huge differences in how humans developed. Some of the dates may not be exact. Looking that far back in time isn't easy, and scientists don't always agree on the meanings of ancient clues.

- 6 million years ago: signs of first humans & how they survived
- 6–3 million years ago: began walking upright
- 2.8–2.6 million years ago: made first tools out of rocks
- 400 thousand years ago: built first shelters
- 200 thousand years ago: modern humans (*Homo sapiens*)—that's us!
- 170 thousand years ago: began wearing clothes
- 100 thousand years ago: invented art and culture
- 12 thousand years ago: discovered farming
- 5 thousand years ago: invented writing
- 3.5 thousand years ago: invented the wheel

[4]What made the biggest difference in how we are today? If you guessed inventing the smart phone, I'm sending you back to the trees. If you guessed learning how to walk instead of <u>loping along on your knuckles</u>, I'll give you part credit. Walking upright freed humans to move beyond the forest in search of food and shelter.

[5]Was making tools the most important? Putting on clothes? Inventing art and culture? Writing? All made huge differences, but I say the number one most important thing humans ever invented was farming.

[6]Farming let people settle down in one place. Instead of spending our lives wandering around hunting for food, we could live at home and grow what we needed. When more of us lived together, we could protect ourselves from attacks by animals and other humans. It was easier to raise children and take care of the sick. We built better <u>shelters</u>, planted crops, and kept <u>livestock</u>. We invented ways to keep records of what we owned. We invented alphabets and writing. The more we invented, the better we got at it.

[7]Today, more than ever we're still exploring, discovering, and inventing. Okay, the cell phone is a cool invention, but farming still gets my vote.

Lesson 4

PARTNER DISCUSSIONS USING THE TEXT "WHAT WAS EARLY HUMANS' GREATEST INVENTION?"

Purpose: To practice determining important information and drawing conclusions.

Part 1. Teacher Prepares Students to Read

Day 1: About 15–20 minutes

Watch with students the video titled "Early Man and His Life" (5:10) or another video that you find appropriate for your students.

https://youtu.be/1S9XZGIupvw

- Organize students into partners.

- Have pairs discuss: *What are recent and past inventions that they think made a great difference in how human beings developed?*

- Ask students to share and write their answers on chart paper under one of these columns: On the left, "Past Inventions;" on the right, "Recent Inventions."

- Give each student a copy of the text and their file folders, and have them retrieve a blank sheet of paper.

Reading the Text

Have students cover paragraphs they're not reading using the blank sheet of paper.

- Explain that *Homo sapiens* is Latin for *wise man* and that humans living today are classified as Homo sapiens.

- Read the first two paragraphs out loud while students follow silently. Ask, *What does the author mean by this last sentence in the second paragraph?* "It took a lot of improvements to take us from playing in trees to playing on cell phones."

- Read Paragraphs three and four and the list of inventions; have students follow silently.

Mention, *The list is the author's top ten. Is there another invention you might add? Explain why.*

- Read to the end as students follow reading silently. Have students turn-and-talk and discuss: What do all these inventions say about us?

- Ask students: *What is livestock?* (Note: Explain if this is an unfamiliar word. Help students understand that livestock—cattle, lambs, sheep, goats, pigs, horses, donkeys, mules—are found on farms.)

Day 2: About 15–20 minutes

Focus on Word Building: Context Clues, Multiple Forms

- Think aloud and model how you use context clues to figure out the meaning of *ancestors* and *roamed* in the sentence: "Apes and people share a common ancestor who roamed around Africa between eight and six million years ago."

- Invite partners to use context to figure out the meaning of *loping along on your knuckles* in the fourth paragraph. Have students explain how they arrived at the meaning.

- Ask students what they know about the word *shelter?* Explain it if students don't know much. Then, invite them to pair-share to discover different kinds of shelter and write their suggestions on chart paper.

- Share these forms of roamed: *roam, roaming, roamed, roamer.* Discuss them. Explain that a roamer is a person who wanders around.

Model Cold Writing in Your Teacher's Notebook

- Use this prompt to jot notes and cold write in front of students. *Creating a system of writing is the most important invention.* (Notes: permanent records for banks, businesses, write letters, reading grew out of writing, leave messages, makes lists as reminders of what to do)

Part 2. Partner Work

Pairs choose two open-ended questions to discuss. Ask students to offer details from the text to support determining important information and drawing conclusions.

Day 3: About 20–25 minutes

- Long ago, animals were stronger than men. How does the text help you know this?

- What does *Homo sapiens* mean? Use information in the text that shows we were and still are *wise.*

- Do you agree with the author, David Harrison, that agriculture is the most important thing humans invented? Explain.

- Discuss three reasons Harrison gives to prove that farming is the most important invention?

- What invention do you think made the biggest difference in our growth as human beings? Give reasons to support your conclusion.

Notebook Writing

Take a few minutes to review the cold writing you modeled for students. Remind them to head a page in their notebook with name, date, and the title of the short text.

- Choose a question you discussed with your partner, write it in your notebook, jot notes, and then put them into sentences.

- Select the invention you believe is most important and jot it in your notebook. List some reasons that support your choice. Organize your reasons into a paragraph with complete sentences.

- Circulate among students to support, observe, and jot notes.

Part 3. Teacher Assesses

- Use your observations and notes along with students' notebook writing.

- Talk to students when you need to clarify your thoughts.

Reflect and Intervene

- On sticky notes, jot what students did well and areas they need support, and then store these in your loose-leaf notebook.

- Help students set a goal for the next guided practice and jot it in their notebook.

Before I Could Write This Poem—

[1]4.5 billion years ago
Earth was born as a fiery ball
from a cloud of gas and dust
circling the sun.

[2]After that—

Earth's surface cooled
into a crust,
and gases from volcanoes
and leaks through the crust
formed an atmosphere
that blocked some of the sun's rays.

[3]So then—

it could rain
and it rained hard and long
and filled the oceans.

[4]Well the crust—

came in pieces
called tectonic plates
and the plates are so big
they carry oceans
and continents on their backs.

[5]It's the tectonic plates—

bumping and grinding
against one another,
that wrinkle up tall mountains,
shake earthquakes,
fling tsunami waves,
and spew volcanoes.

[6]Finally—

plants and animals appeared.
Animals breathe in
what plants breathe out,
oxygen,
and plants breathe in
what animals breathe out,
carbon dioxide.
What a partnership!

[7]Then at long last—

I came along
and grew up and fell in love
and got married
and had two kids
and wrote this poem.

Lesson 5

PARTNER DISCUSSIONS USING THE POEM, "BEFORE I COULD WRITE THIS POEM—"

Purpose: To practice finding main ideas and using details to visualize. Rich in descriptions and images, the poem is ideal for students to create mental pictures of stanzas to deepen their understanding of an event that started 4.5 billion years ago.

Part 1. Teacher Prepares Students

Day 1: About 20 minutes

- Organize students into pairs.

- Give students their folders and a copy of the poem, "Before I Could Write This Poem—"

- Read the poem out loud and have students follow silently.

- Watch a YouTube video that visually shows the Big Bang theory, such as "The Beginning of Everything— The Big Bang" (5:54) https://youtu.be/ wNDGgL73ihY

- As students watch, ask them to link what they see to the first two stanzas of the poem. Discuss with your partner how what you see in the video connects you to these two stanzas.

- Help students learn about the parts of the earth the poem refers to. Put into a search engine: "NASA Cutaway Diagram of Earth's interior" for a good graphic on the NASA website. Explain that the crust is the part of earth we live on and the mantle is made of rock. Point to the core—part of it is liquid iron and inner core is solid iron.

- Have students head a page in their notebooks and draw a diagram of the Earth labeling the crust, mantle.

- Circulate among students to offer support, observe, and take notes.

Day 2: About 20–25 minutes

Focus on Word Building

- Give students their folders and have them retrieve the poem.

- Read the poem out loud and have students follow silently.

- Write these terms on chart paper to introduce students to: *atmosphere*, *tectonic plates*, and *tsunami waves*. Think aloud and show how you use context clues to figure out the meaning of *atmosphere*.

- Have partners read the next three sentences and use context clues to explain each of the underlined words or phrases:

  The Earth's atmosphere is a mixture of gases surrounding our planet giving us air to breath and protecting us from harmful rays of the sun.

  Made of solid rock, tectonic plates are large, irregularly shaped moving pieces in the Earth's crust and upper part of its mantle; all of the earth's land and water sit on these plates.

  Caused by earthquakes or undersea volcanic eruptions, tsunami waves become taller and more powerful as they travel toward land, often at speeds up to 600 miles an hour, producing widespread destruction when they hit land.

- Now show students the National Geographic video "Tsunamis 101" (2:43) or another one you choose. https:// youtu.be/_ oPb_9gOdn4

- Have partners discuss the destructive power of tsunamis and share their thoughts with classmates.

Model Cold Writing in Your Teacher's Notebook

- To find a main idea, tell students you review details in a stanza and ask yourself: *What do these details tell me about the earth?*

- Details in Stanzas 1 and 2: 4.5 billion years ago Earth began as a ball of fire. Its surface cooled and atmosphere developed.

- **Big idea:** It took billions of years for Earth to become a place where we could live and survive.

- Invite students to ask questions so you can clarify their thinking.

Part 2. Partner Work

Day 3: About 20–25 minutes

Partners choose three to four prompts/questions and then discuss details and visualize to better understand the poem.

Prompts/Questions for Paired Discussions

- Partners take turns rereading Stanzas 4 and 5. Discuss the details in each stanza and share the mental picture you create.

- What do you learn about the crust?

- What do you learn about the tectonic plates?

- Find the verbs in the fifth stanza and explain what they have in common? What do the verbs tell you about our earth?

- Discuss the sixth stanza and how plants and animals help one another.

- Find onomatopoeic words that make sounds and discuss how these words add to the pictures the poem paints.

- Why does the poet put himself and his family into the poem's ending?

Notebook Writing

Take a few minutes to review the cold writing you modeled for students. Remind them to head a page in their notebook with name, date, and the title of this selection.

- Choose a stanza, reread it, and use the details to create a mental picture. Draw what you see in your notebook.

- Use the details to think of a big idea for that stanza. Jot the details in your notebook and then write the big idea they help you discover.

- Develop a stanza-by-stanza timeline: Stanza 1, Stanza 2, and so forth. Under each point on the timeline, note the key event.

- Circulate among students to support, observe, and jot notes.

Part 3. Teacher Assesses

- Invite partners to discuss these statements, then write about them in their notebooks:

  The earth can be a dangerous place for people and animals.

  Plants and animals need one another.

- Read notebook entries to see who might require more support to understand these big ideas. Support students who need to revisit and discuss parts of the poem or watch videos again before asking them to revise their notebook writing.

Reflect and Intervene

- On sticky notes, jot what students did well and areas they need support, and then store these in your loose-leaf notebook.

- Help students set a goal for the next guided practice and jot it in their notebook.

Manhunt

Note: I wrote this short, short story in 1966. Twelve editors turned it down. I submitted it to a Writer's Digest writing contest and won a scholarship to a writers' workshop. I came home a better writer and began selling more stories.

Three horsemen—son, father, and grandfather—worked their way across an August brown field studying <u>stirrup-high weeds</u>, looking for, hoping not to find, a body. A <u>covey of quail</u> exploded into the air ahead of them. The son, a pitted faced boy with collar-length hair the color of dirt, threw up his hands like they held a shotgun, clicking his tongue for the number of birds he would have killed. At the end of the field, the boy <u>dismounted</u> and opened a gate. When his father and grandfather had walked their horses through, he followed on foot and shut the gate behind them.

A few yards into the new field, the old man stopped. "Take a break," he said. Moving carefully, he dismounted, lifted his hat, and wiped sweat from his forehead. Holding onto a <u>stirrup</u>, he lowered himself to the ground. His horse walked a few feet away and began grazing. The boy remained <u>sullenly</u> on his horse. His father climbed down and <u>squatted</u> beside the old man.

"Getting tired, Pop?" the boy's father asked.

The old man stared off across the field where half a dozen buzzards drifted aimlessly in the air. "Don't want to find Ed," he said. "Not out here. Not like this."

"We're wasting time," the boy complained.

"We'll be ready when we're ready!" his father snapped without looking up.

"First saw Ed McGrew back when I was cutting hair," the old man went on. "Toughest man I ever knew."

"Never met him," the boy's father said. "Heard stories. About when he was sheriff of Quapaw."

"Probably heard them from me," the old man said. Picking up a stick, he rolled it between his fingers. "One time, two boys in a bar got brave on whiskey, decided to take Ed down."

"Old man McGrew is crazy!" the boy snorted.

"What happened, Pop," the boy's father asked.

"Ed got wind of it," he chuckled. "Came up behind those fellas in an alley."

"You wouldn't believe what we've seen him do!" the boy broke in.

"Ed put 'em both to sleep with the barrel of his pistol," the old man said.

"Bunch of us guys watched him through his window," the boy went on. "He eats dog food!"

"Shut up!" his father said.

"When those boys woke up," the old man chuckled, "they were guests in Ed's jail with bad headaches to show for their trouble."

"Wish I could have known him," the boy's father said.

"He stands in his doorway and pees into the yard!" the boy shouted.

A rider came toward them from the far end of the field. The men removed their hats and stood to wait.

"I'm out spreading the word," the rider said. "We found him. At Pearson's Creek. Had a stringer of perch. Seemed happy to see us. You can go on home."

After the rider left, the old man mounted his horse and sat erect. The boy opened the gate. One by one, in silence, they passed through.

Lesson 6

PARTNER DISCUSSIONS OF THE SHORT NARRATIVE, "MANHUNT"

Purpose: To use the rich dialogue and literary elements to determine personality traits and note the conflicts between and within the characters; to analyze narrative by inferring and making connections. "Manhunt" is a short, short story that will engage readers as they read the reactions of three generations—grandfather, father, and son, all searching for the body of Ed, a former sheriff and legend.

Part 1. Teacher Prepares Students to Read

Day 1: About 20 minutes

- Organize students into partners.

- Have pairs discuss "Manhunt" and generate connotations or associations they nave with the word. (Manhunts are usually associated with searching for criminals.) Write students ideas on chart paper.

- Introduce *covey of quail* and share photographs that show these birds.

- Give each student a copy of the text and their file folders, and have them retrieve a blank sheet of paper.

Reading the Text

- Students cover the dialogue with their sheet of paper.

- Read the first two paragraphs out loud and have students read along silently.

- Have partners discuss the son's actions in the first and second paragraph. Ask, *What do these show about him?* Explain that his actions show that he values hunting, is helpful, feels annoyed, and is impatient. All of these words are personality traits. Explain to students that adjectives are the words we use to show personality traits.

- Read to the end and have students read silently.

- Ask partners to discuss: *Why does Pop admire Ed?* Share with others.

Focus on Word Building: Context Clues, Multiple Forms

- Type into a search engine, "National geographic images of quail"—and share some photos with students. Explain that *covey* is a synonym for *flock* and that a group of quail together is a covey. Ask students: *What in the first paragraph lets you know quail are hunted?*

- Read the sentence with *sullenly*. Explain that it shows the boy's attitude. Help students understand the word and what it shows about the boy's mood.

- Invite partners to read the sentences with these words (first two paragraphs): *dismounted, stirrup, squatted* and use context clues to figure out their meanings. Go back to *stirrup-high weeds* in the first paragraph and ask students how tall the weeds are?

- To help students, find a photo of a horse with saddle and stirrups so they develop a mental image and can estimate how tall the grass is.

- Share forms of squatted: *squat, squatting, squatter.* Discuss the meaning of *squatter* and the term *squatter's rights.* Use the words in sentences to help students understand them.

Model Cold Writing in Your Teacher's Notebook

- Tell students that you'll use the first paragraph and find details that describe the boy's personality traits. Set up you notebook with two columns: On the left write, "The Boy's Traits," and head the right column, "Text Evidence." (Notes: he's a *show-off*—pretends to shoot the quail and count the number he got; he's *helpful* when he dismounts and opens and shuts the gate.)

- Cold write and complete the T-chart.

Part 2. Students Work With a Partner

Discuss all the questions/prompts and cite text evidence to support your thinking.

Day 3: About 25–30 minutes

- Find two to three additional personality traits for the boy in the story.

- Why does Pop admire Ed?

- Why doesn't Pop want to find Ed's body?

- Why does the father wish he knew Ed?

- Why does the son shout insulting phrases about Ed?

- Why does the author title the story "Manhunt?"

- Why does the old man sit erect on his horse after he learns Ed is safe?

- Why does the author have the three walk through the gate "in silence" at the end?

- Why doesn't the author name the grandfather, father, and boy?

Notebook Writing

Take a few minutes to review the cold writing T-chart you modeled for students. Remind them to head a

page in their notebook with name, date, and the title of this selection.

- Choose a question you discussed with your partner, write it in your notebook, jot notes, and then put them into sentences.

- Illustrate a scene in the story.

- Set up a T-chart. Choose a character and identify two personality traits he reveals. On the left write, "Character's Name + Traits"; head the right side with "Text Evidence."

- Circulate among students to support, observe, and jot notes.

Part 3. Teacher Assesses

- Use your observations and notes along with students' notebook writing.

- Talk to students when you need to clarify your thoughts.

Reflect and Intervene

- On sticky notes, jot what students did well and areas where they need support, and then store these in your loose-leaf notebook.

- Scaffold notebook writing using "Manhunt" by supporting students as they turn notes into sentences.

- Help students set a goal for the next guided practice and jot it in their notebook.

The Explorers

[1]What does it take to bet it all—
your life against a chance to win,
to <u>crawl</u> up clouded cold stone peaks,
where ice fields crack and air is thin?

[2]What makes men and women try—
where none has had the nerve before—
to <u>worm down murky</u> canyon walls
and <u>probe</u> the darkest ocean floor?

[3]Who would <u>dare</u> uncharted rivers,
where <u>roaring rapids</u> and <u>brutal piles</u>
of boulders <u>batter</u> the <u>unwary</u>,
with no relief for unmapped miles?

[4]What are astronauts' last thoughts
before they rocket into space?
Do take-off rumbles keep their minds
from life or death they now face?

[5]What drives explorers to the edge
of human limits where they go?
Why do they lay it on the line?
Because we have the need to know.

Lesson 7

PARTNER DISCUSSIONS OF THE POEM, "THE EXPLORERS"

Purpose: To discuss important details such as personality traits; to identify strong verbs and the visualizations they evoke.

Day 1: About 20 minutes

Part 1. Teacher Prepares Students

- Organize students into pairs.

- On chart paper, write this question: *Why do explorers explore?*

- Watch with your students the video: "Age of Exploration" (3:02) or another you select on YouTube.

https://youtu.be/
17OP-2eSW5M

- Ask students to discuss what they recall after watching the video with their partner and share. Have students compare their reasons for exploration with reasons the video explained.

- Give students their folders and a copy of the poem, "The Explorers."

- Read the poem out loud and have students follow silently.

- Reread the poem and ask students to listen for and share the places men and women explored. Jot students' suggestions on chart paper.

Day 2: About 20–25 minutes

Focus on Word Building

- Give students their folders and have them retrieve the poem.

- Explain that the author uses strong verbs to paint pictures in your mind. Reread the first stanza and describe the picture the verb *crawl* helps you create.

- Reread the second stanza and point out the strong verbs *worm down* and *probe*. Help students use context to figure out the verbs' meanings. Then, invite pairs to discuss the mental pictures these verbs develop.

- Introduce these words: *murky, unwary*. Write this sentence on chart paper to show how these words work in a sentence: The <u>unwary</u> mountain climber was unprepared for the <u>murky</u> stretches of rock as he headed toward the mountain's top.

- Reread the third stanza out loud. Invite partners to focus on these words: *dare, roaring rapids, brutal piles, batter, unwary,* and explain the feeling and mood they create. Ask partners to discuss: *What do these words warn explorers of?* (Note: If students find this a challenge, think aloud and show how you use a few of these words to figure out mood. Then, invite students to do the same.)

- Ask volunteers to share their thinking. Encourage others to add their ideas.

- Introduce students to multiple forms of the verb *drives: drive* (base word), *drove, driven, driving, driver*. Discuss each one and use this sentence to show the meaning of: *driven*: The sick child *was driven* to the hospital by her mom.

Model Cold Writing in Your Teacher's Notebook

- Reread the fourth stanza and think aloud noting what astronauts last thoughts might be? Jot these in your notebook. (Notes: Will they live? See family again? Lose contact with space center? Return healthy?)

- Cold write in front of students turning notes into sentences.

Day 3: About 20–25 minutes

Part 2. Partner Work: Partners Discuss the Personality Traits Explorers Need Using Information in the Stanzas

- Partners take turns rereading each stanza out loud and stop to discuss the questions after completing a stanza.

  After rereading the first stanza:

  What personality traits do explorers need to scale mountains?

  After rereading the second stanza:

  What personality traits do explorers need to "worm down" canyons?

  After rereading the third stanza:

  What personality traits allow explorers to boat down rivers no man has explored?

  After rereading the fourth stanza:

  What might astronauts think about before their rocket soars into space?

  After rereading the fifth stanza:

  What drives men and women to explore the unknown?

Notebook Writing

Take a few minutes to review the cold writing you modeled for students. Remind them to head a page in their notebook with name, date, and the title of this selection.

- Choose a stanza, reread it, and use the details to create a mental picture. Draw what you see in your notebook.

- What kind of person sails down miles of an unchartered river or scales mountains or rockets into space? Jot notes that describe the personality of such explorers in your notebook and then turn notes into complete sentences.

- Circulate among students to support, observe, and jot notes.

Part 3. Teacher Assesses

- Read notebook entries to see who might require more support to understand how strong verbs create mental pictures and reveal personality traits. Support students who need to revisit and discuss parts of the poem or watch the video again.

Reflect and Intervene

- On sticky notes, jot what students did well and areas they need support, and then store these in your loose-leaf notebook.

- Scaffold notebook writing using this poem by supporting students as they turn notes into sentences.

- Help students set a goal for the next guided practice and jot it in their notebook.

- Provide intervention for students who need it by re-teaching with a poem or short text in the Appendix.

The Day I Started Becoming an American

[1] We had been at sea crossing the Atlantic more than three weeks. I had been sick almost the whole time. I couldn't keep food down, not even water. I was weak and dirty. My mouth tasted sour. I ached in every joint. It was 1901, and I didn't feel like I'd live to see 1902. I was lying on my stomach with my face buried in my filthy bunk when Mama shook me.

[2] "Hurry, child!" she said. "We're here!" Grasping my hand hard, she helped me up the steep steps out onto the deck. "Look!" she cried. "See the lady? See her standing tall, holding up her torch to welcome us to America? That's the Statue of Liberty, child. We made it!"

[3] Mama was laughing and crying. I cried a little, too. So did a lot of other people crowded around us at the railing. Strangers hugged one another and shouted for joy. I couldn't understand most of the other languages, but I knew they were happy. They waved to the lady as though she could wave back. I was so excited I forgot to be sick.

[4] Our ship docked at a big pier up the Hudson River. Passengers with first and second class tickets got off to move quickly through customs there. The rest of us, who couldn't afford expensive tickets, had made the trip cooped up like animals in the lower decks, where it was always hot and stinky and had no fresh air. Now we were herded onto a barge and taken to an island in New York Harbor near the Statue of Liberty for closer inspection.

[5] When we filed off the barge, we inched in what seemed like an endless line into a huge building and across the biggest room I ever saw. I had read about this place in school back in Ireland. It had many names in the past—Gull Island, Oyster Island, Fort Gibson. When they used to hang pirates here, it was Gibbet Island. Now it was called Ellis Island.

[6] In 1890, President Benjamin Harrison made Ellis Island the first federal immigration station. That was the year I was born! It would have been fun to think that President Harrison did all this just for me, but later, I read that between 1892 and 1954 more than 12 million immigrants—mostly from Europe—entered the United States through Ellis Island.

[7] When it was time for Mama and me, a doctor looked us over to make sure we didn't have a disease we might give to others. He winked at me and said being seasick didn't count. Another man looked at Mama's papers and asked questions to make sure she wasn't in trouble and had a job waiting. She did. We were going to Boston, so Mama could work in a bakery owned by a cousin. We were back on the barge in five hours, crossing the harbor to New York. America was waiting!

Lesson 8

PARTNER DISCUSSIONS OF THE SHORT TEXT, "THE DAY I STARTED BECOMING AN AMERICAN"

Purpose: To make inferences by drawing conclusions; to use details to visualize. This text introduces students to a memoir that recounts the narrator's experiences crossing the Atlantic Ocean to immigrate to America.

Part 1. Teacher Prepares Students to Read

Day 1: About 25–30 minutes

- Organize students into partners.

- Help students understand that a memoir is a collection of significant memories a person writes about his or her life. The memoir is as truthful as the person's memory of events.

- Introduce *immigrant, immigration, immigrate* (base word) and discover what students know about these words. After viewing the video, return to the words and have students discuss their understandings.

- Video: With students, watch the short video, "Ellis Island" (3:30) or another video you select online.

  https://youtu.be/hlHGDw14JZ8

- Have students turn-and-talk and discuss: What did you learn about the people who passed through Ellis Island to live in America from the video? Why did people want to leave their homes and immigrate to America? Why were many immigrants *held* on Ellis island and deported? Why do people visit Ellis Island today?

- Ask students to head a notebook page and jot a list of what they remembered from their discussion.

- Circulate to observe, listen, and take notes to determine how much students remembered.

If necessary, take the time to watch one or both videos again.

- Video: With students, watch the short video, "Tour of a Lifetime of Statue of Liberty" (3:07) or choose a different video on YouTube.

  https://youtu.be/F3wjRQDQnzk

- Have students turn-and-talk and discuss: Why is the Statue of Liberty important to immigrants?

- Have students jot what they recall in their notebooks.

- Circulate among students to support, observe, and jot notes.

Reading the Memoir

- Give students a copy of the memoir and their file folders for storing the texts.

- Read the memoir out loud and have students follow silently.

Day 2: About 20–25 minutes

Focus on Word Building

- Read the second sentence in Paragraph 4 out loud. Think aloud and show students how you use context clues to figure out the meaning of *cooped up*. Say something like: "The author uses a simile to help me—*cooped up like animals in the lower decks*. . . . The phrase like animals makes me think of animals in a cage or chickens in a chicken coop. So cooped up means people in the lower decks were crowded into a small space."

- Invite partners to read the last sentence of the fourth paragraph and use context to figure out the meaning of *herded* and *barge*. Invite pairs to share their process.

- Introduce the terms *symbol* and *symbolize*. Help students understand that a symbol is when one thing represents an idea. For example, the flag symbolizes patriotism and the United States of America, and red is a symbol of blood or the red heart of love on Valentine's Day.

- Introduce other forms of the word *herded*: *herd*, *herds*, *herding* and discuss with students.

Model Cold Writing in Your Teacher's Notebook

- Use this prompt to jot notes and cold write in front of students: *Describe how passengers in the lower decks felt when they "were herded onto a barge and taken to an island . . . "* (Notes: happy to see sky and land; took deep breaths of fresh air; a bit nervous about riding the barge in waves; worried about what would happen on the island)

- Cold write in front of students turning notes into sentences.

Day 3: About 20–30 minutes

Part 2. Partner Work: Draw Conclusions; Visualize

Pairs choose three questions to discuss and offer text details to support their responses.

Prompts for Paired Discussions

- Create a mental picture of what it was like to sail across the Atlantic staying in the lower deck. Use words and your five senses—sight, smell, hear, taste, touch—to describe your picture.

- How does seeing the Statue of Liberty affect Mama and other passengers?

- Draw conclusions about what the trip was like for passengers in cheaper, lower decks? How did they feel about the trip?

- What did the Statue of Liberty symbolize to these people?

- Why did immigrants have to be checked by a doctor?

- Describe the personality traits of the doctor (reread the last paragraph).

- Conclude what thoughts might have gone through the child's mind during the trip? When she and Mama crossed the harbor to New York?

Notebook Writing

Take a few minutes to review the cold writing you modeled for students. Remind them to head a page in their notebook with name, date, and the title of this selection.

- Jot a few notes and then describe what life was like for passengers in the lower deck. Have students put notes into sentences.

- What does the author, David Harrison, mean when he ends the memoir with these three words: "America was waiting!"

- Ask students to select two prompts they discussed. For each one, have them jot a few notes and use the notes to write complete sentences.

- Circulate among students to support, observe, and jot notes.

Part 3. Teacher Assesses

- Use your observations and notes along with students' notebook writing.

- Talk to students when you need to clarify your thoughts.

Reflect and Intervene

- On sticky notes, jot what students did well and areas they need support, and then store these in your loose-leaf notebook.

- Scaffold notebook writing by supporting students as they turn notes into sentences.

- Help students set a goal for the next guided practice and jot it in their notebook.

Ode to the Skunk

[1]It's well you dwell within your skin,
protected from the stink you spout,
while victims hate their fate no doubt—
the agony of breathing in
the fumes of skunkly discontent.

[2]Armed with dreadful, stinkful scent,
marching fearlessly by night,
you frighten enemies to flight,
turn, when vexed, take aim, and vent
on anything that comes too near.

[3]Flaunting famous daunting rear,
you rule the evening woods by fear.

Lesson 9

PARTNER DISCUSSIONS OF THE POEM, "ODE TO THE SKUNK"

Purpose: To make inferences by looking at the skunk from the point of view of other night creatures. To infer, draw conclusions, and enjoy Harrison's playful word inventions such as *skunkly* and *stinkful*.

Part 1. Teacher Prepares Students to Read

Day 1: About 15–20 minutes

- Organize students in partners.

- Have partners turn-and-talk about everything they think they know about skunks.

- Invite pairs to jot their ideas in their notebooks.

- Watch with students the short video, "The Smelly Truth About Skunks" (2:54) or choose another video on YouTube. https://youtu.be/wNGMyaxPItc

- Have partners discuss new information they learned from the video and then jot these facts in their readers' notebooks. Circulate while students write and support those who need your help.

- Collect students' ideas on chart paper.

Reading the Poem

- Give students a copy of the poem and their file folders for storing the poem.

- Read the poem out loud and have students choral read with you

Day 2: About 20–30 minutes

Focus on Word Building

- Have students retrieve the poem "Ode to the Skunk" and the 4 × 6 index card from their folders.

- Remind students to use the index card to cover up stanzas they're not reading.

- Read the first two lines of the poem out loud and show students how you use context to figure out *spout*. Say something like "the stink you spout" is what the skunk does—so *spout* is another word for spray.

- Invite partners to use context and information from the video to figure out the meaning of *fumes*, *vexed*, *vent*, and *flaunting*, and have them share what they discovered. If students have difficulty, use the word in a sentence that shows it's meaning and write the sentence on chart paper. Then have students determine meaning.

- Introduce these forms of *fumes*: *fume*, *fumigate*, *fuming*, *fumed*, and discuss the meaning and function of each word in a sentence, such as the following: The <u>fumes</u> from the smoke made firefighters cough. The pest control company will <u>fumigate</u> the house to rid it of bedbugs. <u>Fuming</u>, Jack refused to sit in the time out chair. Jack <u>fumed</u> as he thought about being grounded for a week.

Model Cold Writing in Your Teacher's Notebook

- Use this question to jot notes and cold write in front of students: *Why do skunks "march fearlessly by night?"* (Notes: spray enemies; enemies fear the spray's stink; stink hard to get rid of)

- Cold write in front of students turning notes into sentences.

Day 3: About 20–30 minutes

Part 2. Partner Work: Draw Conclusions

Pairs choose two open-ended questions to discuss. Ask students to offer details in the poem and from the video to support their answers.

Prompts for Paired Discussions

- Why do victims of a skunk's spray hate being sprayed?

- How can other creatures avoid being sprayed by a skunk?

- Why do skunks attack?

- How are skunks helpful?

- Explain what the poet, David Harrison, means by the last two lines of the poem. Why does he close the poem this way?

- How do the invented words *skunkly* and *stinkful* make you feel about *discontent* and *scent*? Why do you think the poet chose to play with the words *skunk* and *stink*?

Notebook Writing

Take a few minutes to review the cold writing you modeled for students. Remind them to head a page in their notebook with name, date, and the title of this selection.

- Ask students to select two prompts they discussed. For each one, have them jot a few notes and use the notes to write complete sentences.

- Have students explain why they think Harrison wrote the last two lines of this poem by first, jotting a few notes and then putting notes into sentences.

- Circulate among students to support, observe, and jot notes.

Part 3. Teacher Assesses

- Use your observations and notes along with students' notebook writing.

- Review forms of *fume* and ask students to explain how each one can be used.

- Review words students explained using context clues: *vexed, vent, flaunting*, and ask them to return to the poem and use context to explain the meaning of each word.

Reflect and Intervene

- Scaffold notebook writing using this poem by supporting students as they turn notes into sentences.

- Re-teach vocabulary words that students have difficulty explaining.

I Am Not a Number

[1]Last night the weather was warm and the stars were out, so Mom and my little sister and I slept outside on blankets spread on the grass. Mom told Molly her favorite bedtime story about a mouse that finds a strawberry. It was too dark to read, but Mom can't read well anyway so she always tells her stories. I've heard the mouse and the strawberry about a thousand times, so I thought about other stuff, like how full I was. We'd stood in line at the church for box dinners and ate them in our car with the doors open. I would get a free breakfast at school today so finding food wasn't on my mind.

[2]I thought about how lucky I am. No one has messed with my sister or me. Mom protects us, and we love her. I thought about my homework. My life is <u>complicated</u>. Sometimes, just the little things take longer than expected. I'm a guy, so if nature calls, and I'm not close to an indoor toilet, I've been known to step behind a tree somewhere to do my business. Molly is only three, so it doesn't matter as much for her. But for Mom it's a different thing. Some nights it takes forever to find a restaurant or filling station or just somewhere that allows the public to use their bathrooms.

[3]After that, we like to go to the park so Molly can run and get some exercise while we wait for the food line to open over at the church. Before we lost our last apartment, it didn't take Mom long to open a can of stew or make sandwiches or even cook a full meal. Now that we're back to living in the car, things are harder. It's not like we're broke or anything. Mom has a little money in her purse. We get welfare, and once in a while Mom's dad comes by and gives her ten dollars or whatever he can spare. Then, we go to the grocery store and stock up on food that won't spoil. Lots of nights we eat right out of those boxes and bags. That doesn't sound like we have any manners. We do, but when you're eating in a car, there's not much room for manners.

[4]Anyway, if I don't get my homework done before it gets dark, I'm screwed. And last night it got dark before I was ready. Mom started a new job. She says soon we'll find another apartment. That would sure help. I'm falling farther and farther behind in school. The other day, I saw a newspaper headline that said almost one kid in every ten is homeless. That makes me a number: I'm that one kid. But I don't feel like a number. I feel like me, a real person who is having a hard time for now. I can do better. I want to. One of these days, when things get better, I will.

Lesson 10

PARTNER DISCUSSIONS FOR THE TEXT, "I AM NOT A NUMBER"

Purpose: To make inferences to identify personality traits, draw conclusions, and visualize. This memoir builds empathy and compassion for homeless families with children.

Part 1. Teacher Prepares Students to Read

Day 1: About 20 minutes

- Organize students into partners.

- Watch the video, "Positively Homeless: Homelessness in America" (5:01) ▶

  https://youtu.be/j32IEpYvqvA

- Invite students to turn-and-talk about the hardships of homelessness from the children's point of view—from the parents' point of view. Why is it important to help families who are homeless find work and a home?

- Have pairs discuss: What might make a teenager say, "I am not a number?"

- Review *memoir* so students understand it's a biography that a person writes based on his or her memory of significant events. It's based on the person's memories and perceptions of events.

- Give each student a copy of the text and their file folders, and have them retrieve the blank sheet of paper and cover paragraphs not being read.

Reading the Text

- Read the first two paragraphs of the memoir out loud and ask students to follow silently.

- Stop after the second paragraph, share your emotions, and explain why.

- Read the last two paragraphs of the memoir out loud and have students follow silently.

- Have partners turn-and-talk and share their feelings along with parts of the text that caused these emotions.

Focus on Word Building: Context Clues

Day 2: About 15–20 minutes

- Reread the second paragraph out loud. Then read the sentence: "My life is complicated."

- Have partners discuss details in this paragraph that explain the meaning of *complicated*. Students share.

- Introduce the words *complicate*, *complicating*, and *complication*. Explain that *complication* is a noun. Write this sentence on chart paper or a whiteboard: Losing their apartment and becoming homeless created <u>complications</u> for this family, such as sleeping outside or in a car. Ask students to use context clues in this sentence to explain complications.

Model Cold Writing in Your Teacher's Notebook

- Use this prompt to model cold writing: *The narrator's mom does the best she can for her son and daughter.* (Notes: Mom tells bedtime stories, she makes sure kids get dinner at church, and they play and get exercise in the park.)

- Cold write in front of students turning notes into sentences.

Part 2. Students Work With a Partner

Day 3: About 20–25 minutes

Prompts for Paired Discussions

Pairs choose two questions that ask them to use text details to draw conclusions. Encourage students to reread or skim parts of the memoir to find evidence and paraphrase it in their words.

Prompts/Questions for Paired Discussions

- Discuss why the memoir is titled: "I Am Not a Number."

- What are two personality traits of Mom? Use text details to support your thinking.

- What are two personality traits of the narrator? Use text details to support your thinking.

- Skim Paragraphs 1, 2, and 3. Choose one paragraph, reread it carefully, and describe the picture the details create in your mind.

- Explain why the ending of the memoir is hopeful by citing text details.

Notebook Writing

Take a few minutes to review the cold writing you modeled for students. Remind them to head a page in their notebook with name, date, and the title of this selection.

- Choose a question you discussed with your partner, write it in your notebook, jot notes, and then put them into sentences.

- Explain why the narrator dislikes the newspaper headline. Jot notes and then put them into sentences.

- Use *complicated* and *complication* in sentences that show you understand their meaning.

- Circulate among students to support, observe, and jot notes.

Part 3. Teacher Assesses

- Return to the chart where students offered suggestions prior to reading the memoir for what made a teenager say, "I am not a number." Invite students to add to or refine ideas now that they've read the memoir.

- Read students' notebook entries and reflect on how students did adjusting the statement, "I am not a number." Make a list of students who require extra support and practice.

Reflect and Intervene

- Decide how you will support students who required interventions: work with a peer; scaffold specific areas using this text or re-teach using a text in the Appendix I.

Now . . . and Then

[1]Look around your classroom. What do you see? How many kids are there? Are you all in the same grade? About the same age? Is there a hallway outside your door? Other rooms? Other grades? Other teachers? Does your school have a library? An all-purpose room? A nurse? Custodian? Secretary? Principal? How many kids go to your school? How do they get there?

[2]Go back in time 130 years and pretend you are going to school in 1890. Now look around your room. You see a teacher, the same as now. A teacher's desk and desks for students—also like now. Maybe a chalkboard, wastebasket, pegs for hanging jackets, shelves for storing books, and sack lunches . . .

[3]. . . sack lunches? Well sure, if you want to eat. The lunchroom? It's at your desk or on the playground. See those horses grazing in the field? One of them is yours. That's how you get to school and back. While you're out there, should nature call, you'll be close to the privy. Indoor plumbing? Think of it as outdoor plumbing. Smells bad? Aww.

[4]By now you've noticed that your whole school is one room. There are eight grades, one teacher, and not another soul. First graders sit up front. Eighth graders sit in the back. You are taught reading, writing, arithmetic, history, and geography. The big kids help the little ones, unless they're busy chopping wood or hauling in coal to keep the stove going in cold weather. Your teacher gets to school early to sweep the floor and light the fire, so the room will be clean and warm by the time you arrive. Hot weather is easier. Air-conditioning? If you're too warm, teacher will open a window.

[5]If your one-room schoolhouse feels too big and fancy, go back a little earlier. Abraham Lincoln, who was born in 1809, didn't see much of any kind of school. He had less than one year of formal education, and it came in snatches of time now and then. Even so President Lincoln managed to hold our country together during the worst time in our history. George Washington was born in 1732. As a boy, he may have had some tutoring and limited time in a local school, but when he grew up, he saved our young nation during the Revolutionary War and became our nation's first president. When Benjamin Franklin, perhaps the most brilliant American of his time, was a kid around 1711, he had two years of schooling. Everything else that Ben learned, that George learned, that Abe learned, they taught themselves by reading, learning, and working.

[6]Students today have more comforts, bigger schools, and more choices than kids had in the old days. But one thing has never changed. Good students have always learned how to read, learned how to learn, and kept learning over a lifetime. In the end, learning isn't about buildings. It's about time and how we spend it.

Lesson 11

PARTNER DISCUSSIONS OF THE SHORT TEXT "NOW . . . AND THEN"

Purpose: To compare and contrast to show how two things are alike and different. To learn about what school and education was like for students who lived 130 to 300 years ago.

Part 1. Teacher Prepares Students to Read

Day 1: About 20–25 minutes

- Organize students into partners.

- Watch with students the short video "One-Room Schoolhouses in America" (3:32) or any other that you think is appropriate for your kids. (Note: Be prepared to read aloud the captions in this video.)

  https://youtu.be/AoieZKCVm-w

- Have students turn-and-talk and use these questions to discuss what they learned from the video: What did you notice about the one-room schoolhouses you saw? How would you compare the rooms you saw to your classroom? Who did the one teacher teach? How did stagecoaches and then buses change where students went to school?

- Ask students to jot a list of points they recalled in their notebooks. (Note: Rewatch the video if students need to improve recall.)

- Circulate among students to support, observe, and take notes.

Reading the Text

- Give students a copy of the text and their file folders for storing the poem.

- Read the text out loud and ask students to follow silently.

- Introduce compare and contrast as a way to show how two different things are alike and different.

- Model comparing and contrasting using a Venn diagram (see Appendix E).

- Think aloud to show students one way their school is like and one way it's different from one-room schoolhouses: alike: study the same subjects; different: students are organized by grade.

Day 2: About 15–20 minutes

Focus on Word Building

- Read the third paragraph out loud and have students follow.

- Ask partners to turn-and-talk and use context clues to explain *privy*.

- Introduce other words for *privy*: outhouse, latrine, cow shed, Johnny Blue.

- Have partners turn-and-talk and use context clues to explain *hauling*.

- Review compound words using schoolhouse as an example.

- Invite pairs to turn-and-talk and find three examples of compound words from their background knowledge. Write on chart paper what students share.

Model Cold Writing in Your Teacher's Notebook

- Use this prompt to jot notes and cold write in front of students: *Learning in a one-room schoolhouse was difficult.* (Notes: Students in Grades 1–8; older students taught younger ones; had to chop wood and haul coal to keep warm in winter; bathroom outside)

- Cold write in front of students turning notes into sentences.

Part 2. Partner Work: Compare, Contrast, Visualize

Day 3: About 15–20 minutes

Pairs choose two questions to discuss and provide details from the text to support their ideas.

Prompts for Paired Discussion

- Reread Paragraphs 1–3 and show how your school is alike and how it differs from a school in 1890.

- Why was a one-room schoolhouse difficult for the one teacher? How could it be easier for the teacher?

- What does the one room schoolhouse tell you about the world children lived in?

- What does your school tell about the world you live in?

- How did the work students did in the one-room schoolhouse differ from what you do in your school? Why do you think these differences exist?

- How did Abe Lincoln and Ben Franklin become educated?

- Explain what the author means when he writes: "In the end, learning isn't about buildings. It's about time and how we spend it."

- Visualize or create a mental picture of a one-room schoolhouse in the winter or spring. Use words to describe what you see to your partner.

Notebook Writing

Take a few minutes to review the cold writing you modeled for students. Remind them to head a page in their notebook with name, date, and the title of this selection.

- Give students a copy of a Venn diagram (Appendix E). Share what you modeled on the first day.

- Have them work independently to complete the diagram.

- Partners can share their diagrams with each other.

- Circulate among students to support, observe, and take notes.

Part 3. Teacher Assesses

- Use your observations and notes along with students' notebook writing.

- Talk to students when you need to clarify your thoughts.

- To support your assessments, consider having students complete part or all of the self-evaluations and discussing it with them during a short conference.

Reflect and Intervene

- On sticky notes, jot what students did well and areas they need support, and then store these in your loose-leaf notebook.

- Scaffold students' Venn diagram work on comparing and contrasting using this text.

- Help students set a goal for the next guided practice and jot it in their notebook.

FIGURE 3.7: SEVENTH GRADER HELENA'S COMPARE/CONTRAST GOES BEYOND A LIST OF FACTS.

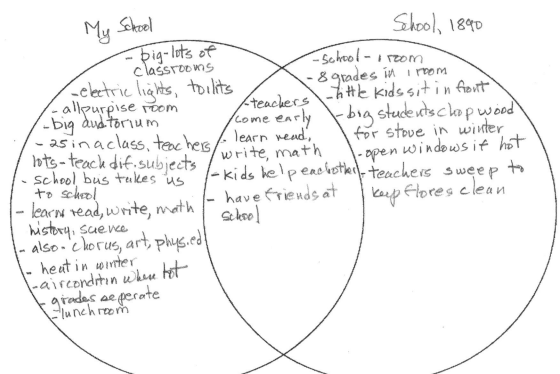

My School

School, 1890

- big-lots of classrooms
- electric lights, toilits
- allpurpise room
- big auditorium
- 25 in a class, teachers lots - teach dif. subjects
- school bus takes us to school
- learn read, write, math history, science
- also - chorus, art, phys. ed
- heat in winter
- aircondidin when hot
- grades seperate
- lunch room

- teachers come early
- learn read, write, math
- kids help eachother
- have friends at school

- school - 1 room
- 8 grades in 1 room
- little kids sit in front
- big students chop wood for stove in winter
- open windows if hot
- teachers sweep to keep flores clean

There's more to do in my school than one in 1890. We learn more subjects and have Chrome books. Learning & helping important in 1890 & my school.

If Stones Had Tongues

(Story of Stonehenge)

[1]On Salisbury Plain
giant stones form a ring
like a gathering of silent elders.

If only

[2]stones had tongues to tell
of men five thousand years ago
with tools simple as antlers
who dug deep trenches here,

of how

[3]two thousand years later
men with strong wills
pried from rock beds
stones weighing tons and dragged them—
no matter how or how far—
to Salisbury Plain.

If only stones

[4]had tongues to tell what the ancients meant,
why for fifteen hundred years
they kept at it . . .

adding . . .

changing . . .

rearranging . . .

[5]until at last it—whatever it was—
was done,
or they quit.

Did these stones guard

[6]the dead at rest in nearby fields?
Were they bridges
from this world to the next?
On Salisbury Plain
the elders hold their silence.

If only

[7]stones had tongues.

Lesson 12

PARTNER DISCUSSIONS USING THE POEM, "IF STONES HAD TONGUES"

Purpose: To have students use details to visualize, make inferences, and determine main ideas. To introduce students to the fascinating story of Stonehenge.

Part 1. Teacher Prepares Students to Read

Day 1: About 25–30 minutes

- Organize students into partners.

- Video: With students, watch the short video "The History of Stonehenge for Kids: Stonehenge for Children" (3:37), or select another video. (Note: You might want to watch the video twice as there's lots of information for students to recall.)

  https://youtu.be/wf7xwHFuH2o

- Put into a search engine: "Map of England Showing Stonehenge." Select a map and point out that Stonehenge is on Salisbury Plain, southwest of London.

- Invite partners to discuss the video. Ask: *Where is Stonehenge located? How many years ago did people start building it? How much does the largest stone weigh? What was used to dig the deep trenches or ditches? What do scientists think Stonehenge might have been used for?*

- Have students jot a list of details they recall from their partner discussions in their notebooks.

- Circulate to observe, listen, support, and take notes. Then, have students share.

Reading the Poem

- Give students a copy of the poem and their file folders for storing the poem.

- Read the poem out loud and have students read silently.

- Have students use the video and the poem to discuss with partners: Why do you think visitors go to Stonehenge?

Day 2: About 15–20 minutes

Focus on Word Building

- Introduce the term *tons* and tell students there are 2,000 pounds in a ton.

- Reread the second stanza and have students choral read it with you. Ask them to figure out the meaning of *trenches* using clues in the last line.

- Invite partners to discuss the meaning of the title: "If Stones Had Tongues." Have them share thoughts.

Model Cold Writing in Your Teacher's Notebook

- Use this prompt to jot notes and cold write in front of students: *Explain what Harrison means in the first stanza: "On Salisbury Plain/ giant stones form a ring/like a gathering of silent elders."* (Notes: tells the arrangement, size, and location of stones; compare them to a group of silent elders—this points to their age—elders—and the mystery—the stones can't talk so we don't know much about them.)

- Cold write in front of students turning notes into sentences.

Part 2. Partner Work: Visualizing, Making Inferences, Determining Main Ideas

Pairs discuss recall questions. Then choose two to three open-ended questions to discuss. Ask students to offer details in the poem they used to answer questions.

Prompts for Paired Discussions

- What details do you learn in the third stanza? (recall)

- What information do you learn in the fourth stanza? (recall)

- Use the details to develop a mental picture and explain what you see to your partner.

- What are the two mysteries surrounding Stonehenge?

- Make inferences, using details, about the people who built Stonehenge four to five thousand years ago.

- Have partners use the guidelines to discuss main idea. Find one to two main ideas in the poem by doing the following:

  Select details.

  Use the details to figure out the general topic.

  What is most important about the topic?

  Write that as your main idea.

Notebook Writing

Take a few minutes to review the cold writing you modeled for students. Remind them to head a page in their notebook with name, date, and the title of this selection.

- Ask students to select two prompts they discussed. For each one, have them jot a few notes and use the notes to write complete sentences.

- Have partners discuss the mysteries surrounding Stonehenge and develop a theory that could solve each one. Then, students jot notes based on their discussion and turn notes into clear sentences.

- Circulate among students to support, observe, and take notes.

Part 3. Teacher Assesses

- Use your observations and notes along with students' notebook writing.

- Talk to students when you need to clarify your thoughts.

Reflect and Intervene

- On sticky notes, jot what students did well and areas they need support, and then store these in your loose-leaf notebook.

- Scaffold notebook writing using this poem by supporting students as they turn notes into sentences.

- Help students set a goal for the next guided practice and jot it in their notebook.

CHAPTER 4

Shared Reading Lessons

Jennifer Harrison's fourth graders enjoy reading aloud "George Washington Carver."

The emphasis in the shared reading lessons is on using open-ended questions to interpret sections of the text. During shared reading, the teacher listens to students' responses carefully and notes their answers plus text support on a pre-prepared anchor chart. After completing a lesson, students reread the poem or short text and their responses on the anchor chart to make adjustments and add extra ideas. Students also do some notebook writing, discussing with a partner, and practice applying strategies such as inferring, compare/contrast, visualizing, and finding themes.

George Washington
American Revolutionary War
1775–1783

The Man for the Job

[1]Imagine fighting the British Empire,
going to war to win your freedom,
risking your life and all you own.
They knew they didn't dare lose.
They had to find the right leader.
It was all over if the wrong side won.

[2]Some shouted YES! Some shouted NO!
Farmers with <u>muskets</u> against trained forces?
The leader would face an impossible task!
Facing a polished, powerful <u>foe,</u>
he could not win—yet must not lose.
Where was that man? Who could they trust?

[3]George. George. His name was repeated,
till the man for the job accepted his fate,
as well as the fate of a new nation.
He promised to train this <u>ragtag</u> army,
build its strength, teach it to fight,
see to its clothing, weapons, rations.

[4]George, George, the man for the job,
led them through seven years of misery—
weary men, bitter defeats,
troops so hungry they boiled their boots—
told his wolf-thin frozen army
they'd whip the Brits. They would succeed.

[5]And then the day at Yorktown came.
The British, surrounded, surrendered at last.
Cannons grew hushed, the bloodshed stopped.
We'd paid dearly, but won our freedom.
When all seemed hopeless and lost, we'd won,
thanks to George, the man for the job.

Lesson 13

SHARED READING OF THE POEM, "THE MAN FOR THE JOB"

Purpose: To help students practice recalling details, inferring, drawing conclusions

Lesson Materials:

- Copies for all students of the poem, "The Man for the Job"

- Students' file folders for storing short texts; 4 × 6 index card for covering stanzas

- Map of original 13 colonies and a world map

- An anchor chart headed with the title of the poem. Write *colonies, colonists,* and this sentence: *Before we became Americans, there were thirteen <u>colonies</u> ruled by England; people living in the colonies were called <u>colonists</u>.* Discuss meanings of these words with students.

- Make two columns on the anchor chart: Title left side "Inference" and right side "Text Evidence."

- Video: "George Washington—First U.S. President" (4:45), or go to YouTube.com and find another. https://youtu.be/hvE9fb--Dig

- Read the poem aloud to students and have them take turns reading it aloud to their partner.

- Students will paraphrase details in a stanza to demonstrate recall.

- Students will infer why George was "the man for the job" and the personality traits George had that made him the best person for the job.

Day 1: About 20 minutes

Part 1. Pre-Teach

- Watch the YouTube video about George Washington.

- If you prefer, ask your librarian to recommend a picture book about George Washington and read it to students.

- Ask students to share what they learned about George Washington from the video.

- Review the meanings of *colonies* and *colonists* on the anchor chart. Post on a whiteboard a map of the 13 colonies.

- Post a world map to show the distance between England and the colonies. Discuss what problems the distance might pose to both.

Day 2: About 30 minutes

Part 2. Start the Shared Reading Lesson

Have students pair-share for questions that ask them to infer and draw conclusions.

- Read the title and the first two stanzas out loud. Students follow silently.

- Ask students to discuss the following questions:

First Stanza:

    Who were the colonists fighting?

    What were the colonists fighting for?

    Infer: Why was it important that the colonists find the "right leaders"?

Second Stanza:

    Did everyone want to fight the British? How does the author show that?

    What kind of an enemy were British soldiers? Can you give words and phrases from the stanza to show this?

    Use clues in the sentence to explain what a musket is: "Farmers with muskets against trained forces?"

    Who is the "foe?" What does foe mean?

- Read stanzas three and four out loud. Students read silently.

- Ask students to discuss the following questions:

  Third Stanza

  What did George promise?

  Read the last three lines of the third stanza and use context to figure out what "ragtag" army means.

  Infer what "accepted his fate" means.

  Fourth Stanza

  What was the seven years like for the "troops?" Give examples from this stanza.

  Draw conclusions about how the troops must have felt about George.

  Fifth Stanza

  Why did the British surrender at Yorktown?

  How do you feel when you read "Cannons grew hushed, the bloodshed stopped."

  Infer what "we paid dearly" means.

Wrap Up: Notice how well students recalled details, found evidence in the text, could infer, and draw conclusions.

Day 3: About 15 minutes

Part 3. Teacher Assesses

Complete the Anchor Chart

Additions and adjustments come from the students. You'll want to see what they can add. If they add little, then students might be telling you they require more practice. You can redo part of the lesson or move on and slow down, checking frequently for understanding.

- Ask students to retrieve the poem from their folders.

- Reread the poem and invite students to choral read with you.

- Reread the chart notes and invite students to add or adjust details.

- Review *colonists* and *colonies*; introduce the base word, *colony.*

Reflect and Intervene: On sticky notes, jot the names of students who didn't participate or contribute ideas for the anchor chart. Work with individuals or a small group. Return to modeling and then invite students to respond.

Jane Goodall: A Portrait of Determination

¹In June 1960, Jane Goodall climbed from a boat 4,300 miles from London where she was born and stood at the edge of a wild forest in Tanzania, Africa. Trees and thick underbrush crowded the shore and covered the steep hills beyond. She had been sent to this <u>remote</u> place by the great scientist Louis Leakey to study chimpanzees. Jane had loved animals all her life but she had no college degree and no field experience with chimpanzees. She faced a daunting task.

²It was her love for animals and adventure that first led Jane to Kenya, Africa, where, by chance, she became Louis Leakey's secretary. When she went with him on a field trip to search for ancient pre-human bones, Leaky liked what he saw in her—patience, a keen eye for observation, and a willingness to work alone. That's why he chose her to go to the Gombe Stream Reserve in Tanzania to study chimpanzees.

³Jane's mother and an African cook made the journey with her across Tanganyika, the world's second deepest lake, but her mother would only stay a few months. Jane and the cook would remain. After making camp Jane set out into the <u>vast</u> forest to locate chimps. Armed with a notebook and binoculars, she finally located a troop in the distance, but they spotted her and disappeared into the trees when she was still 500 yards away—the distance of four football fields placed end to end.

⁴She must have felt discouraged, but the patience and determination Louis Leakey had seen in Jane gave her the courage to set out again. Day after day, she walked alone through the forest, listening, watching, and recording what she observed. At last she found a second group of chimps. Unlike the first group, these chimps kept their distance but didn't run away.

⁵Each day Jane appeared in the same spot where the chimps could look at her while she looked at them. It took an entire year before the chimps allowed her to come within thirty feet of their feeding area. This was a <u>huge breakthrough</u>. No other scientist had been so close to chimpanzees in the wild. Jane named them instead of using numbers as other researchers had. A second year passed as she sat patiently on the jungle floor, climbed trees, ate some of the same food the chimps ate, watched, listened, and recorded.

⁶The chimps accepted Jane. They came to her for bananas. They visited her camp. As years passed, she learned that chimpanzees sometimes hunt and eat meat, throw stones, and make tools by forming twigs and grass into probes to pull out termites for snacks. They may go to war with neighboring troops. They have a vocabulary using sounds, play tricks, show affection, sadness, and tenderness.

⁷Jane Goodall studied chimpanzees for 26 years. Thanks to her heroic efforts in a Tanzanian forest, today we have a far better understanding about chimpanzees, our closest non-human relatives.

Lesson 14

SHARED READING OF THE SHORT TEXT, "JANE GOODALL: A PORTRAIT OF DETERMINATION"

(Note: The poem about Jane Goodall from Lesson 1 and this text can stand on their own. However, reviewing the poem enriches students' learning.)

Purpose: To practice discussion of open-ended questions that have more than one answer; to practice determining important information and recalling details

Lesson Materials:

- Copies for all students of the short text, "Jane Goodall: A Portrait of Determination"

- Students' file folders for storing short texts; a blank sheet of paper for covering paragraphs

- An anchor chart headed with the title of the text. Write these vocabulary words on the chart leaving room for students' explanations: *remote, vast, huge breakthrough.*

- Write *determination* and this sentence: *Rosa's determination to win the race helped her deal with the hard training.* Then write *determine, determined, determining.*

- Write the lesson's questions on the chart and leave space to note students' responses.

Day 1: About 20–30 minutes

Part 1. Pre-Teach

If necessary, watch the video from Lesson 1 again, or you might want to watch the video titled "Jane Goodall Tribute" found on YouTube.

https://youtu.be/06M7hggEz7k

- Introduce *determination* along with *determine, determined, determining.* Show how you use context clues to figure out the meaning of determination.

- Make sure students know what a *portrait* is. If not, explain by showing them portraits on the Internet.

- Read "Jane Goodall: A Portrait of Determination" out loud and have students follow by reading silently.

Day 2: About 30 minutes

Part 2. Start the Shared Reading Lesson

After each pair-share, invite students to share their thinking and make clear that you want different ideas and different evidence from the text. Note students' thoughts on the anchor chart.

- Organize students into partners.

- Have students use the blank sheet of paper in their folders to cover up part of the text they're not reading.

- Read paragraphs one and two out loud; students read silently.

- Ask students to figure out the meaning of *remote* by finding clues in sentences one, two, and three.

- Have students pair-share to respond to these questions and find more than one reason. They'll need text details to support their thinking. *Why does the author write that Jane faced a daunting or difficult task? Why did Leaky, a famous scientist, choose Jane to study chimps?*

- Have students cover up Paragraphs 5–7. Read Paragraphs 3 and 4 out loud; students read silently.

- Ask partners to discuss and find text evidence for these questions: *Why does Jane feel discouraged? How do you know chimpanzees are shy and unused to human beings?*

- Read to the end of the selection; students read silently.

- Have students work independently and use details in Paragraph 5 to define *huge breakthrough*.

- On their own, ask students to answer these questions and find texts details to support their positions: *How do you know the chimps accepted Jane? Why was it important for Jane to learn about chimps?*

- Ask students: *Why did the author David Harrison title this "A Portrait of Determination?"*

Wrap Up: Notice how well students used context clues, worked with a partner to discuss questions, and worked on their own to answer questions.

Day 3: About 15–20 minutes

Part 3. Teacher Assesses

Complete the Anchor Chart

Additions and adjustments come from the students. You'll want to see what they can add.

If they add little, then students might be telling you they require more practice. You can redo part of the lesson or move on and slow down, checking frequently for understanding.

- Have students retrieve the text from their folders.

- Reread the text and ask students to follow silently.

- Reread notes on anchor chart and have students add or adjust notes.

- Review *remote*, *vast*, and *breakthrough*.

- Have students offer text details t*o support the* title: "Jane Goodall: A Portrait of Determination."

Reflect and Intervene: On sticky notes, jot the names of students who weren't discussing with a partner and had a tough time citing text evidence. You can intervene with individuals or a small group and model how you return to the text to respond to a question, and then have students respond using a different question.

Rain, She

[1]Rain, she watch jungle.
Oh yes!
Rain, she slyly lift each leaf,
tiptoe down trunk of kapok tree,
make sure jungle nice and green.

[2]Rain, she know when jungle thirsty.
She bang on forest roof,
plunk rubber trees on their heads.
"Wake up! Drink!" she say.
Oh yes!
Rain, she plump up blossoms,
make them nice and fancy for thirsty bees.

[3]Rain, she not forget animals!
Oh no!
She drench fur of sullen jaguar,
make parrots shake their feathers,
drip off howler monkey's nose.
Oh yes!

[4]And rain, she never never forget
to pelt and rattle thatch huts,
drip through cracks, trickle down walls.
"Ha!" she say. "This I do for you.
I keep river full, fish happy,
I pour your squash a drink."

[5]Then rain, she say,
"This I do for me.
I keep jungle nice and green.
Oh yes!"

Lesson 15

SHARED READING OF THE POEM, "RAIN, SHE"

Purpose: To understand how personification and onomatopoeia enhance meaning and support visualizing

Lesson Materials:

- Copies for all students of the poem, "Rain, She"

- Students file folders for storing short texts; 4 × 6 index card for covering stanzas

- An anchor chart headed with the title of the poem. Post both sentences on anchor chart: <u>Personification</u> is giving non-living things the ability to do what humans can do. David Harrison <u>personifies</u> rain by making it a woman who cares for the rainforest.

- Make two columns on the anchor chart. Title left side "Strong Rain Verbs" and title right side, "What You Picture."

- Video: "Rain Forests 101/ National Geographic" (3:41) or another video about rain forests that's appropriate for your students.

https://youtu.be/ 3vijLre760w

Day 1: About 15–20 minutes

Part 1. Pre-Teach

- Watch video "Rainforests 101/National Geographic." (You might want to watch this twice). Invite students to share all they remember. Discuss *green canopy* and *ecosystems*.

- Show photo of the Kapok tree. Have students look at the person compared to the size of the tree. Connect Kapok tree to the green canopy and point out the animals that live in the tree and connect that to ecosystems. A great online resource can be found here: https:// www.istockphoto.com/photos/kapok-tree?me diatype=photography&phrase=kapok%20 tree&sort=best

- Ask students to head a page in their notebooks and explain what the *green canopy* of the rainforest is and why it's important. Circulate and help students by answering questions or helping them frame responses.

Day 2: About 15–20 minutes

- Give students a copy of the poem and read the poem out loud. Have students read silently.

- Read the sentences on the anchor chart for personification and personifies. Model how you use clues to figure out the meaning of *personification*. Invite students to explain *personifies* using sentence clues.

- Have students turn-and-talk and discuss the meaning of these words using context clues.

- Reread the title and ask students to explain how David Harrison personifies rain.

- Reread the poem and ask students to turn-and-talk and find other examples of rain being personified as a woman.

- Introduce *onomatopoeia* and explain that words that also create sounds are onomatopoeic words. As an example point to *bang* in the second stanza. Ask, *What kind of noise does bang make?*

- Have students find other words in the poem that also make sounds: *plunk, shake, pelt, rattle.*

Day 3: About 20–30 minutes

Part 2. Start the Shared Reading Lesson

- Have students retrieve a copy of the poem "Rain, She" and the 4 x 6 index card from their folders. Students use their index cards to cover up stanzas three to five.

- Read Stanzas 1 and 2 out loud. As students follow silently, have them spot words that show what *she* does.

- Have students turn-and-talk, share words, and write these on the left side of the anchor chart.

   First and Second Stanzas

   How do these words (watch, tiptoe, bang, plunk, drink, plump up) help you see and hear what she is doing? Tell students these are strong verbs because they paint pictures and create sounds.

   What other words in Stanzas 1 and 2 relate to water?

- Read aloud the rest of the poem and students read silently.

   Third Stanza

   What does she do for animals? What words show you this?

   Which words are onomatopoeic words?

   Fourth Stanza

   How are people in the huts feeling about "rain, she?" Use details from the poem to support your ideas.

   How does the rain help people?

   Last Stanza

   Why does rain say, "This I do for me." How do these words link to what the poet is saying about rain in the rainforest?

- What affect does repeating "oh yes!" have on your feelings? On the poem's meaning?

- Reread each stanza. Turn-and talk about the picture you see in your mind and the words

and phrases that helped create these. Share with the class.

Wrap Up: Notice what students did well: finding strong verbs, onomatopoeic words, visualizing, and offering text details.

Day 4: About 15 minutes

Part 3. Teacher Assesses

Complete the Anchor Chart

Additions and adjustments come from the students. You'll want to see what they can add. If they add little, then students might be telling you they require more practice. You can redo part of the lesson or move on and slow down, checking frequently for understanding.

- Have students retrieve the poem from their folders.

- Ask students to choral read as you reread the poem.

- Review anchor chart notes and have students make adjustments and add ideas.

- Review *green canopy, kapok tree, personification,* and *personify* and connect to the poem.

Reflect and Intervene: On sticky notes, jot the names of students who didn't participate or contribute ideas for the anchor chart. Work with individuals or a small group. Return to modeling and then invite students to respond.

FIGURE 4.1: FIFTH GRADER, AUDREY, ILLUSTRATES "STRONG RAIN" VERBS.

FIGURE 4.2: FIFTH GRADER, MYA SELF-EVALUATES USING CONTEXT CLUES TO FIGURE OUT VOCABULARY.

The Service Dog

Man's Best Friend

[1]Ichito is eight years old. One night he almost died. They saved his life in the emergency room at the hospital. He is highly allergic to peanuts so he must be on guard at all times to keep from accidentally eating some. He is safer now. He has a service dog trained to smell peanuts. If Ichito is about to put food in his mouth that has peanuts in it, his dog moves between him and his food and refuses to let him eat it.

[2]Johnson suffers epileptic seizures. One might happen anytime, anyplace. He doesn't worry quite as much now because his service dog is trained to bark for help if he has a seizure when he's alone. His dog can also bring his medicine and even a phone when Johnson is coming out of a seizure.

[3]When we say dogs are man's best friends, there are good reasons, especially when an owner has a disability and needs help 24 hours a day. Service dogs are not the same thing as comfort dogs. Some people need the comfort of their beloved pets near them when they are traveling, shopping, or doing other tasks that make them tense. Most comfort animals are dogs, but a variety of species have shown up as comfort pets, including parrots, pigs, ferrets, and even cats and mice.

[4]True service animals are always dogs, and they are trained for one to two years before they are ready to help their owners deal with physical or emotional challenges. Whether training is done by a professional or at home, it takes time and patience by both the animal and its trainer to prepare for a lifetime of service. All the time, fees, health care, and registrations make service dogs cost from $15,000 to $30,000, and some are much more expensive.

[5]Most of us have seen service dogs at work guiding people who are blind about their daily business. Trained dogs have been performing those services for centuries. Other dogs are trained to help their owners who have hearing problems by alerting them to sounds around them and leading them away from danger. For someone who has trouble getting up and down, a service dog is trained to bring needed items. Service dogs have learned how to press buttons to open doors or turn lights off and on and to perform other tasks that make life easier. There are dogs trained to save people with diabetes by smelling changes in their blood sugar level and alerting them in time to take their medicine. The list of what dogs do for people is amazing and long. For just about every human need, a dog can be trained to help. Service dogs are far more than pets. They are working animals that have gone to school and graduated with the skills they need to serve a specific owner with a specific need. They are truly man's best friend.

Lesson 16

SHARED READING OF THE SHORT TEXT, "THE SERVICE DOG: MAN'S BEST FRIEND"

Purpose: To make inferences and understand the author's purpose

Lesson Materials:

- Copies for students of the short text, "The Service Dog: Man's Best Friend"

- Students' file folders for storing short texts; a blank sheet of paper for covering paragraphs

- An anchor chart headed with the title of the text. Explain *diabetes* and *epileptic seizures* to students. Write these vocabulary words and sentences on the chart leaving room for students' explanations: *refuses, centuries. My brother* <u>refuses</u> *to play with his younger sister. For* <u>centuries</u>, *hundreds of years, men have hunted wild animals for food and clothing.*

- Write the lesson's questions on the chart and leave space to note students' responses. On the left side write "Questions"; on the right side write "Student Responses."

Day 1: About 25–30 minutes

Part 1. Pre-Teach

- Watch the YouTube video, "Meet The Puppies Training To Be Service Dogs" (10:33). It's long but really offers students big insights.

  https://youtu.be/mW1-SbxTQiU

- Ask students to turn-and-talk and discuss what they learned about training service dog puppies from watching the video. Students share.

- Have students head a page in their notebooks and write a list of what they learned about training service dog puppies. Circulate and support students.

- Explain that to make an inference you use information in a text to find unstated meanings. For example, I can infer that trainers remove puppies that aren't making enough progress because people's lives are in the dogs' hands.

- Invite students to turn-and-talk and make a different inference based on the video.

- Use context clues in the sentences on the chart to have students figure out the meaning of each one.

- Introduce students to other forms of *refuse*, discuss each, and use *refusal* in a sentence to show its meaning: *refuse, refused, refusing, refusal.*

- Read "The Service Dog" out loud and have students follow silently.

Part 2. Start the Shared Reading Lesson

Day 2: About 20–30 minutes

After each pair-share, invite students to share their thinking and make clear that you want different details from the text. Note students' thoughts on the anchor chart.

- Have students use the blank sheet of paper in their folders to cover up part of the text they're not reading.

- Read paragraphs one and two out loud and have students follow silently. Ask students to answer questions and offer text details as support.

  How does Ichito's service dog help him?

  How does John's service dog help him?

  Using both stories, make an inference about service dogs.

- Read Paragraphs 3 and 4 out loud and have students follow silently. Ask students to answer questions and offer text details as support.

  Make an inference that shows why most service animals are dogs.

  Why are service dogs expensive?

  Why do service dog trainers need patience?

- Read the last paragraph and have students follow silently. Ask:

  Share three things service dogs do to help people.

  Explain this statement from the text: "Service dogs are far more than pets."

  Make an inference about the training of service dogs.

Wrap Up: Notice how well students could use details to draw conclusions.

Day 3: About 15–20 minutes

Part 3. Teacher Assesses

Complete the Anchor Chart

Additions and adjustments come from the students. You'll want to see what they can add.

If they add little, then students might be telling you they require more practice. You can redo part of the lesson or move on and slow down, checking frequently for understanding.

- Have students retrieve the text from their folders.

- Review vocabulary.

- Organize students in partners and give each pair a sticky note and ask them to write their names at the top. Have each pair choose a word, discuss its meaning, and on the sticky note, use it in a sentence to show their understanding. Post sticky notes on chart paper and have pairs volunteer to read their sentences.

- Invite students to add details to the anchor chart.

Reflect and Intervene: On sticky notes, jot the names of students who didn't participate or contribute ideas for the anchor text. Work with individuals or a small group using one of the extra pieces provided in the Appendix.

Lost and Found

Note: Ryan Speedo Green found himself in a juvenile detention center when he was twelve because he was unable to control his rage. However, by tapping into his strong determination to change his life and by accepting the help of others, he became a Metropolitan Opera Star.

[1]He thought back to the kid he used to be—

a small black <u>volcano</u> of a boy—

who erupted out of control when he was twelve.

Life at home kindled the fire of rage.

At school he swore at his teacher, threw his desk.

She tried to help but he didn't know how to accept.

[2]Outburst by outburst he ran toward certain ruin.

He threatened lives, was led away in <u>shackles</u>,

screamed and screamed until he could scream no more.

It was over, unless he could find another way.

He promised himself he was better than that,

promised himself to save himself,

He began at last to listen to those who could help.

[3]It was a miracle people didn't give up on him,

but they saw more than a little boy filled with hate.

Today he stars in the Metropolitan Opera.

His voice booms out in bass and baritone,

those long-ago screams replaced by a passion to sing.

From <u>solitary confinement</u> to a world stage,

the lost is found, the boy is proud of the man.

Lesson 17

SHARED READING OF THE POEM, "LOST AND FOUND"

Purpose: To apply protagonist, problems, and antagonists to a narrative poem to deepen students' understanding; cause and effect

Lesson Materials:

- Copies for all students of the poem, "Lost and Found"

- Video: "Opera Singer Defies Odds to Become Promising Star" (5:52) or another online video about Ryan Speedo Green of your choosing https://youtu.be/gNeed2jo3No

- Students file folders for storing short texts; 4 × 6 index card for covering stanzas

- An anchor chart headed with the title of the poem. On the chart, write these three sentences with vocabulary from the poem. Students will use context clues and background knowledge to figure out word meanings: 1) The <u>volcano erupted</u> and fire and melted rock poured out of the top and flowed down its sides. 2) The prisoner wore <u>shackles</u> on his feet and hands to prevent an escape. 3) In a prison, <u>solitary confinement</u> means the prisoner is alone in a small cell.

- Make two columns on the anchor chart. On the left side write, "Literary Elements" and list protagonist, problems, and antagonists. Head the right side, "Text Evidence." Leave space between terms for text evidence students offer.

- Title the back of the anchor chart "Cause/Effect." Make two columns. On the left write "Cause"; on the right write "Effect(s)."

Day 1: About 20–25 minutes

Part 1. Build Background Knowledge

- Teach cause/effect. Say, *Your room is a mess. Mom inspects it. What are the effects?*

Note students' responses on the board. Then, explain that a cause can be an event, what a person says or does, the weather, or inner thoughts. The effect is one or more results that grow out of the cause.

- Watch the video and ask students to think of cause/effect in Ryan's life.

- Ask students: *What did you learn about Ryan Speedo Green? What did he do to change the direction of his life? What do you think about his singing?*

- Explain to students that *opera is a play with the character*s singing to each other and themselves instead of talking.

- How else is opera like a play?

- Using the video, help students identify cause and effect in Ryan Speedo Green's life.

  Give students this cause: Ryan throws his desk at his teacher, Betty Hughes. Have students turn-and-talk to find effects.

Day 2: About 15–20 minutes

Pre-Teach

- Give students their folders and a copy of the poem, "Lost and Found"; read the poem out loud. Have students read silently.

- Read the first sentence with "volcano erupted" on the anchor chart. Think aloud to show students how you used clues in the sentence to figure out meaning.

- Organize students into partners.

- Ask pairs to read the second and third sentences on the anchor chart and use context clues to figure out the meaning of the underlined words. Have students share and take the time to discuss each word.

- Introduce: *erupt, erupted, erupting, eruption.* Point out that *erupt* is the base word from which other forms derive. Explain that words that end in *-tion* are always nouns, like *eruption.* Use each form in a sentence and write sentences on the whiteboard. Discuss with students.

Day 3: About 20–25 minutes

Part 2. Start the Shared Reading Lesson

- Give students their folders and have them retrieve their copy of the poem, "Lost and Found" and their 4 × 6 index card.

- Read the title and the first and second stanzas out loud and ask students to follow silently.

- Ask students to answer the following questions using text details to support their ideas.

    First Stanza:

    What do you learn about the protagonist and his problems in this stanza? What do you imagine happened to Ryan when you read: "Life at home kindled the fire of rage"? How is Ryan an antagonist working against himself? Use clues in the stanza to describe what kind of a boy Ryan was.

- Read aloud the second stanza and have students read silently.

- Ask students to answer the following questions using text details to support their ideas.

    Second Stanza:

    Why was Ryan put in shackles? What are his problems now? What were his antagonists in this stanza? How does he start changing his life?

- Read aloud the third stanza and have students read silently.

- Ask students to answer the following questions using text details to support their ideas.

    Third Stanza:

    How does Ryan change his life? Explain the meaning of the last two lines and link them to the first two stanzas. Why do you think Ryan changed his life? What messages or themes about life and decisions does this poem send to you?

- Invite students to turn-and-talk to find a cause statement and resulting effects in Stanzas 2 and 3. Students share. (Notes: If students need support, review the work you did with students on cause/effect under Part 1, Day 1. Think aloud using the line, *"Life at home kindled the fire of rage"* as a cause. The effects are, he was out of control at 12, swore at his teacher, threw a desk.)

Wrap Up: Notice what students did well: identifying problems, discussing antagonists, and identifying cause/effect.

Day 4: About 15–20 minutes

Part 3. Teacher Assesses
Complete the Anchor Chart

Additions and adjustments come from the students. You'll want to see what they can add. If they add little, then students might be telling you they require more practice. You can redo part of the lesson or move on and slow down, checking frequently for understanding.

- Have students retrieve the poem from their folders.

- Have students choral read as you reread the poem.

- Ask students to reread the anchor chart and add notes to problems and antagonists. Also, ask them if they see additional messages or themes in the poem. Add these to the chart.

- Review vocabulary: *erupt, erupted, erupting, eruption.*

- Review cause/effect and ask students to share an example from the poem.

Reflect and Intervene: On sticky notes, jot the names of students who didn't participate or contribute ideas for the anchor chart. Work with individuals or a small group. Return to modeling and then invite students to respond.

FIGURE 4.3: FIFTH GRADER, MYA, IDENTIFIES LITERARY ELEMENTS FOR THE POEM "LOST AND FOUND" AND ILLUSTRATES HER UNDERSTANDING OF VOCABULARY.

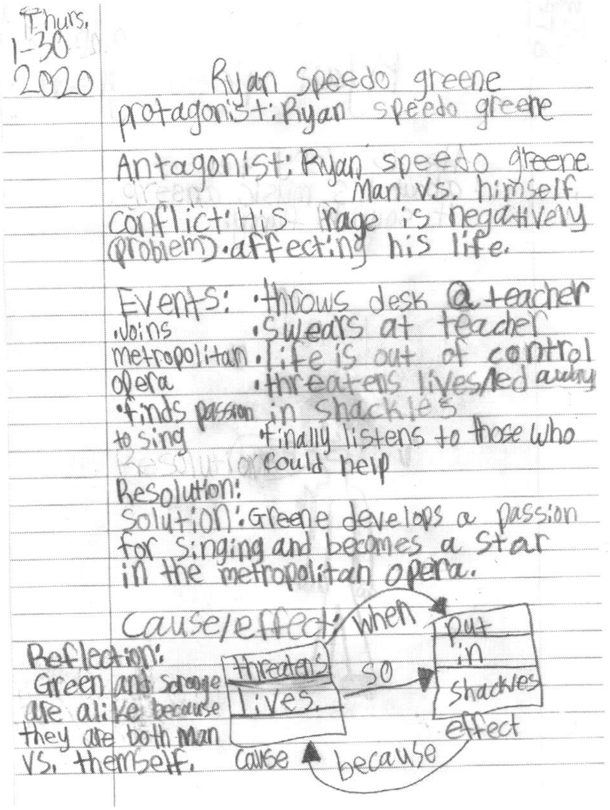

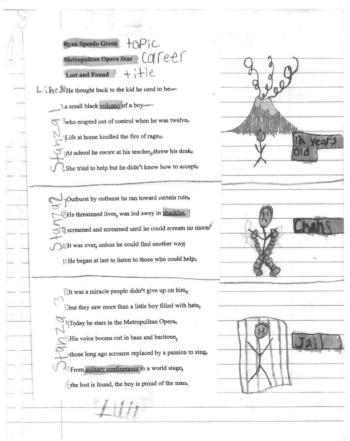

Thurs.
1-30
2020

Ryan speedo greene
protagonist: Ryan speedo greene

Antagonist: Ryan speedo greene
Man vs. himself
conflict: His rage is negatively
(problem) affecting his life.

Events: · throws desk @ teacher
· joins   · swears at teacher
Metropolitan · life is out of control
opera   · threatens lives/led away
· finds passion in shackles
to sing   · finally listens to those who
                could help

Resolution:
Solution: Greene develops a passion
for singing and becomes a star
in the metropolitan opera.

Cause/effect: when   put
                        in
Reflection: threatens so shackles
Green and scrooge lives.
are alike because   effect
they are both man   cause ← because
vs. themself.

Ryan Speedo Green topic
Metropolitan Opera Star career
Lost and Found + title

Line 1 He thought back to the kid he used to be
2 a small black volcano of a boy
3 who erupted out of control when he was twelve.
4 Life at home kindled the fire of rage.
5 At school he swore at his teacher, threw his desk.
6 She tried to help but he didn't know how to accept.

7 Outburst by outburst he ran toward certain ruin.
8 He threatened lives, was led away in shackles.
9 screamed and screamed until he could scream no more.
10 It was over, unless he could find another way.
11 He began at last to listen to those who could help.

12 It was a miracle people didn't give up on him,
13 but they saw more than a little boy filled with hate.
14 Today he stars in the Metropolitan Opera.
15 His voice booms out in bass and baritone,
16 those long ago screams replaced by a passion to sing.
17 From solitary confinement to a world stage,
18 the lost is found, the boy is proud of the man.

Lili

(margin labels) Stanza 1 · Stanza 2 · Stanza 3

(illustration labels) 12 years old · Chains · Jail

Johnny Appleseed—Jonathan Chapman

One Man—Two Stories

Johnny Appleseed

[1]As the legend goes, there once was a poor young man from a large family in Massachusetts who struck out on his own, walking barefooted and headed west. At a cider mill he filled a bag with free apple seeds that he began to plant along his journey.

[2]He sold seeds and sprouts to pioneers who were also headed west to start new lives. If they had no money, he traded sprouts for food or clothes. If they had nothing to trade, he gave them sprouts so the families would have juicy apples to eat when they got settled. Folks began calling the young man Johnny Appleseed.

[3]Stories about Johnny Appleseed spread. One time, he met a band of rough men in the woods who wanted to fight him. Johnny bet them he could chop down more trees than they could. He won his bet and planted apple seeds on the land they'd cleared. Mama bears trusted him so much they would watch Johnny wrestle their cubs.

[4]Johnny Appleseed dressed in rags and carried his cooking pot on his head. He walked all his life, rarely wore shoes, never had a home, and planted his apple seeds all the way across the country to California. His feet were as tough as an elephant's hide, so tough a rattlesnake couldn't bite through. He could melt ice with his feet and leap across rivers. And did you know he slept with bears to keep warm on winter nights? Well that's what folks said. Johnny Appleseed was quite a guy!

Jonathan Chapman

[5]Johnny Appleseed was a real man, but his name was Jonathan Chapman. It's true he was born in Massachusetts (on September 26, 1774). After his mother died when he was young, his father remarried and had ten more children. The family was poor. Food must have been scarce and the Chapman house noisy and crowded. When John was 22, he left home for good and walked westward, the same direction many pioneer families were going.

[6]The story is true up to that point. But John Chapman was far from being a happy hobo scratching out a living selling apple seeds and sprouts. He was developing a business. He started by using free apple seeds from cider mills to plant a nursery in Pennsylvania. Apples from those seeds were not the kind to eat or use in cooking. They were small and bitter and made good hard cider, an alcoholic drink that many pioneers liked to keep on hand.

[7]As he walked as far west as Illinois and north to Ontario, Chapman bought land in Ohio and Indiana and planted more nurseries. He hired people to run his businesses and moved on. Now and then he would come back to check on things.

[8]When Chapman died on March 18, 1845, in Indiana, he owned 1,200 acres of land. Maybe Johnny Appleseed's story was more fun, but Jonathan Chapman became a wealthy man.

Lesson 18

SHARED READING OF THE SHORT TEXT, "JOHNNY APPLESEED–JONATHAN CHAPMAN: ONE MAN–TWO STORIES"

Purpose: To compare and contrast the real person and the legend, as well as the problems each faced; visualize using text details

Lesson Materials:

- Copies for students of the short text, "Johnny Appleseed—Jonathan Chapman: One Man—Two Stories"

- Students' file folders for storing short texts; a blank sheet of paper for covering paragraphs

- An anchor chart headed with the title of the text. Write these vocabulary words and phrases on the chart leaving room for students' explanations: *sprouts, scarce, nurseries.*

- Write the lesson's questions on the chart and leave space to note students' responses.

https://youtu.be/
bg6wXWOINyc

- Video: "Johnny Appleseed," visuals by Verne Andru (2:06)

Day 1: About 20–25 minutes

Part 1. Pre-Teach

- Watch with students the YouTube video: "Johnny Appleseed" visuals by Verne Andru.

- Discuss the term *legend* and have students discuss what in the video is part of the legend about Johnny.

- Organize students into partners. Invite pairs to discuss these questions: *What kind of a person was Johnny Appleseed? Why did Johnny help pioneers who were traveling West? Why did Johnny wear a pot as a hat? How did Johnny feel about living in the woods without a gun?*

- Give each student his or her folder and a copy of the story.

- Have students retrieve the sheet of paper to cover up paragraphs during the shared reading lesson.

- Read aloud the short text, "Johnny Appleseed" and have students follow silently, while they cover up "Jonathan Chapman."

- Read aloud "Jonathan Chapman" and have students follow silently.

Day 2: About 20–30 minutes

Part 2. Start the Shared Reading Lesson

After each pair-share, invite students to share their thinking and use details from the text to support their ideas. Note students' thoughts on the anchor chart.

- Organize students into partners. Remind them to use text details to support answers.

- Reread aloud "Johnny Appleseed" and have students choral read with you.

- Ask students: *What parts of Johnny Appleseed are exaggerations? What kind of person was Johnny? Why do you think stories about Johnny Appleseed spread? How do you picture Johnny Appleseed?*

- Reread "Jonathan Chapman" and have students choral read with you.

- Ask these questions, urging students to use the text to find details to support their responses:

  ○ *How do you know food was scarce? Why do you think John left home at 22? How does Chapman's life differ from the legend of Johnny Appleseed?*

  ○ *Why did John Chapman become a wealthy man? Which do you prefer and why: the legend or the true story? What kind of a person was John Chapman?*

- Compare and contrast: *Were Johnny Appleseed and John Chapman alike in any ways? How were they different?*

Wrap Up: Notice how well students used details to visualize and compared Appleseed to Chapman.

Day 3: About 10–15 minutes

Part 3. Teacher Assesses
Complete the Anchor Chart

Additions and adjustments come from the students. You'll want to see what they can add. If they add little, then students might be telling you they require more practice. You can redo part of the lesson or move on and slow down, checking frequently for understanding.

- Have students retrieve the text from their folders.

- Review vocabulary.

- Invite students to reread notes on the anchor chart and add or adjust details.

- Introduce tall tales, stories with exaggerated details. Have students explain why "Johnny Appleseed" is a tall tale.

Reflect and Intervene: On sticky notes, jot the names of students who didn't participate or contribute ideas to the anchor chart or who might need additional support with comparing and contrasting and figuring out what kind of person the legend and the real Johnny were. Work with individuals or a small group using one of the extra pieces provided.

George Washington Carver (1864–1943)

[1]A poor child,
born a slave
before the Civil War.

[2]Kidnapped.
Sold.
Lost his mother.
What chance did he have?

[3]Loved art, science, plants.
<u>Determined</u> to go to school.
Studied soybeans,
sweet potatoes,
peanuts,
<u>rotating crops</u>.

[4]Became a scientist,
inventor, teacher.
Helped farmers
feed their families
like no one before.

[5]Became famous.
<u>Respected</u> by presidents,
world leaders.
Had his face on a stamp,
his name on a ship.

[6]George Washington Carver
made the world a better place.
Each of us is richer because
of that poor child.

Lesson 19

SHARED READING OF THE POEM, "GEORGE WASHINGTON CARVER"

Purpose: To use details to make inferences and determine important information such as personality traits

Lesson Materials:

- Copies of the poem, "George Washington Carver," for each student

- Students file folders for storing poem. Have students retrieve the 4 × 6 index card for covering up stanzas

- An anchor chart headed with the title and author of the poem. Write these vocabulary words on the chart and leave room for students' explanations: *determined, rotating crops, respected.*

- Prepare the anchor chart for you to write students' ideas. Make two columns: Left side titled "Personality Traits" and right side titled "Supporting Text Details."

- Video: "George Washington Carver: Scientist & Inventor/ Mini-Bio" (4:29), or choose another video online. https://youtu.be/ sdz8XTNttdc

Day 1: About 20 minutes

Part 1. Pre-Teach

- Watch video and have students discuss these questions: *Why was getting an education difficult? What do you learn about his interests and talents from the video? What words could describe Carver's desire for an education?*

- Give students a copy of the poem, "George Washington Carver."

- Read aloud the poem and have students read silently.

- Read aloud the third stanza and show how you figure out the meaning of *determined* using context clues.

- Have students read the fifth stanza and use context clues to figure out the meaning of *respected.*

- Help students understand the meaning of *rotating crops* in the third stanza. Explain: To keep soil in fields rich, farmers plant different crops in the same field and follow a pattern of changing crops annually or every other year.

- Introduce multiple forms of *determined*: *determine* (base word), *determining*, *determination* (noun, ends in *-tion*). Discuss the words; use them in sentences so students understand more about each one.

- Teach the difference between physical traits and personality traits. Students need to understand the difference to experience success with the poem.

Day 2: About 20–30 minutes

Part 2. Start the Shared Reading Lesson

After each turn-and-talk, invite students to share their thinking and make clear that you want different details from the text. Note students' thoughts on the anchor chart.

- Organize students into partners.

- Have students use the index card in their folders to cover up stanzas not being read.

  First and Second Stanzas:

    Read the title and the first two stanzas, and have students follow reading silently.

Why does the poet ask: What chance did he have?

What feelings do you think George Washington Carver's childhood created in him? Explain.

- Read Stanzas 3 and 4, cover the last two stanzas. Students read silently.

Third and Fourth Stanzas:

Reread the words that show what Carver studied. Ask: Using what Carver studied at school, predict using text details what you think he'll become.

Is "determined" a personality trait? Explain.

How does being a scientist connect to growing soybeans, sweet potatoes, and so forth?

What do the lines, "Helped farmers/ feed their families/like no one before" tell you about Carver's personality?

What else do you learn about Carver's personality traits from information in both stanzas?

Fifth and Sixth Stanzas:

Read both stanzas out loud and have students follow silently.

How do you know Carver became famous?

Explain the meaning of "respected" using details to support your thinking.

Reread Lines 1 and 2 of the last stanza. What personality trait do these lines suggest?

Reread the last two lines out loud. Have students pair-share and discuss what the author means.

What personality traits help a person change and reach a dream?

Wrap Up: Notice all the positives students did during the lesson: listening carefully; identifying personality traits and finding supportive text details; figuring out the meanings of words.

Day 3: About 10–15 minutes

Part 3. Teacher Assesses

Complete the Anchor Chart

- Give students their folders and ask them to retrieve the poem, "George Washington Carver."

- Reread the poem and invite students to choral read with you.

- Review vocabulary, including forms of determined.

- Read each personality trait and evidence and ask students if they want to add details or a new trait and details.

Reflect and Intervene: Reflect on students' responses and decide who might benefit from extra support with vocabulary and/ or identifying personality traits. Work with individuals or a small group using one of the extra pieces in the Appendix to re-teach personality traits.

The Masters of Pollination

[1]When flowers open in spring, their pollen ripens. Pollen comes from the male part of the plant. To become fertilized (pollinated), the pollen must reach the female part, called the stigma. Since plants can't walk they need help to make this happen. Nature has given them a way. The plants make sweet nectar. Lots of creatures like nectar, including butterflies, beetles, and birds. But the all-time queen of pollination is the honeybee.

[2]The honeybee makes honey from nectar and gets protein by eating pollen. When pollen catches a ride on the bee's hairy body, some shakes loose on the plant's stigma and fertilizes it. The bee doesn't know this is happening or do it on purpose. But this happy accident makes honeybees important to humans. Without honeybees, we humans would suffer! As much as one third of what we eat is made possible because bees are so good at what they do.

[3]Farmers count on honeybees to fertilize their crops. The list of food that bees help provide includes about 130 plants in the United States, such as almonds, apples, avocado, green beans, blackberries, cantaloupes, cherries, onions, peaches, pears, strawberries, tomatoes, and watermelons.

[4]Some crops are so huge there aren't enough local bees to handle the job. Beekeepers may be called on to haul their bees around the country where they can do the most good. When almond trees blossom in California, enough honeybees are needed to visit billions of flowers in 60 days. It takes roughly twelve hundred thousand hives of bees to pollinate all those blossoms.

[5]Hauling billions of bees about the country is hard work and timing is important. With the tupelo gum trees of Florida, beekeepers' bees have about three weeks to finish pollination. Alfalfa, one of the most important sources for honey, blooms for a week or so. In the United States, there are about 27 million acres of alfalfa—about the size of Maryland, Hawaii, Massachusetts, and Vermont put together. Some citrus flowers are finished in two or three days. Cotton flowers last a day. Lettuce blossoms open after daybreak and close forever before noon. When a job is done, keepers load their hives and truck them off to their next job.

[6]Bees are insects with brains the size of this period. They don't know they are working for us. They are simply gathering food to feed their brood. They don't know how much they mean to us, but we know. We know what honeybees need to survive. They need protected places to live, plenty of plants they like, and time to just be bees. We need to be careful with the sprays we use and leave more blooming weeds and wildflowers along fencerows, roadsides, and edges of pastures. The better we take care of the masters of pollination, the better they can take care of us.

Lesson 20

SHARED READING OF THE SHORT TEXT, "THE MASTERS OF POLLINATION"

Purpose: To determine important information in a text and draw conclusions; to identify problem and solution

Lesson Materials:

- Copies for all students of the short text, "The Masters of Pollination"

- Students file folders for storing short texts; 4 × 6 index card for covering stanzas

- An anchor chart headed with the title of the text. On the chart, write these words: *fertilize, nectar, haul, brood.* Leave space to note meanings.

- On the anchor chart, leave space for recording students' responses. Add the two columns with headings: "Bees" on the left and "Draw Conclusions" on the right.

- Video: Watch with your students "Bee Pollination—A Beautiful Natural Act" (2:22), or choose another video online.

https://youtu.be/
9Zbq3KB4MpI

Day 1: About 15 minutes

Part 1. Build Background Knowledge

- Watch the video: "Bee Pollination—A Beautiful Natural Act."

- Ask students to discuss: *What did you learn about nectar from the video? Why do bees start gathering pollen from the male flower first? Why is pollination important?*

- Give students a copy of the short text, "The Masters of Pollination" and their folders.

- Read the entire selection out loud. Students read silently.

- Organize students in partners and have pairs discuss amazing facts they learned about bees from the text and video. Share with the class.

Day 2: About 15–20 minutes

Pre-Teach

- Give students their folders and have them retrieve the short text, "The Masters of Pollination."

- For *fertilize,* read the first and second paragraphs out loud. Explain to students that it was helpful to read the second paragraph to gather more information about *fertilize.* Think-aloud and explain its meaning using all the clues. Help students understand that fertilize is a synonym for pollination.

- Organize students in pairs. Invite pairs to read the sentences with *nectar, haul,* and *brood* and use context clues to figure out the meaning of each word. Have students share. If students find this challenging, return to thinking-aloud until they *get it.*

- Introduce students to multiple forms of *pollination: pollinate* (base word), *pollinating, pollinated, pollinator.* Point out that *pollination* is a noun (words ending in *-tion* are nouns) and *pollinator* refers to the bee who pollinates by visiting many flowers. Use words in sentences and invite students to help you compose them.

Day 3: About 25–30 minutes

Part 2. Start the Shared Reading Lesson

- Give students their folders and have them retrieve their copy of "The Masters of Pollination" and the blank sheet of paper for covering up paragraphs.

- Read Paragraphs 1–3 and have students choral read with you. Ask: *How has nature helped bees want to pollinate? Why are honeybees important to people? Why do farmers need bees?*

- Read Paragraphs 4–5 and have students choral read with you. Ask: *Why do beekeepers have to haul their hives around the country? Why is timing important for having bees pollinate crops? Why is pollinating the alfalfa crop in the United States a challenge each year?*

- Read Paragraph 6 and have students choral read with you. Ask: *Why is the survival of honeybees important?* <u>Draw conclusions</u> *about why people need bees? Draw conclusions about how people harm bees? Draw conclusions about why people need to take care of bees. What does the author mean by the last sentence in this paragraph?*

- Why did the author, David Harrison, title this piece "The Masters of Pollination?"

- Identify the problem Harrison raises. What are some possible solutions?

Wrap Up: Notice how well students could draw conclusions, figure out word meanings using context clues, figure out and discuss the meaning of the title and the last line of the sixth paragraph.

Day 4: About 15–20 minutes

Part 3. Teacher Assesses

Complete the Anchor Chart

Additions and adjustments come from the students. You'll want to see what they can add. If they add little, then students might be telling you they require more practice. You can redo part of the lesson or move on and slow down, checking frequently for understanding.

- Have students retrieve the text from their folders.

- Ask students to reread the anchor chart and add notes to the "Drawing Conclusions" section. Also, ask them if they see additional ways of dealing with the problem of a shortage of bees. Add these to the chart.

- Review *pollinate, pollination, pollinating, pollinated, pollinator.*

Reflect and Intervene: On sticky notes, jot the names of students who didn't participate or contribute ideas for the anchor chart. Work with individuals or a small group. Return to modeling and then invite students to respond.

Amazon Rain Forest

¹The Amazon flows flat, brown, and wide,
For four thousand miles before it's done,
Through trees that crowd the banks on either side.

²While undergrowth provides a place to hide,
And high above the monkeys have their fun,
The Amazon flows flat, brown and wide.

³Young men along the Amazon take pride
In learning how to hunt with dart or gun
Through trees that crowd the banks on either side.

⁴This far upstream from distant ocean tide,
When monsoons come you seldom see the sun
As rivers rise higher, brown, and wide.

⁵Somewhere a jaguar pads with silent stride.
Eyes bright its hunt has just begun
Through trees that crowd the banks on either side.

⁶No one could walk it all, no one has tried.
Of bigger rainforests there are none.
The Amazon flows flat, brown, and wide
Through trees that crowd the banks on either side.

Lesson 21

SHARED READING OF THE POEM, "AMAZON RAIN FOREST"

Purpose: To use details to determine main idea, make inferences, and visualize

Lesson Materials:

- Copies for all students of the poem, "Amazon Rain Forest"

- Students' file folders for storing short texts; 4 × 6 index card for covering stanzas

- Put into a search engine, "Map of Amazon River." Select a map to share with students on a whiteboard. Discuss: *What continent is the Amazon River on? What countries does the river run through? Where does the river start and end? What do you think people use the Amazon River for?*

- An anchor chart headed with the title of the poem. Write repeated line: "Through trees that crowd the bank on either side" on the chart.

- Make two columns on the anchor chart: Title left side "Main Idea" and right side "Text Evidence."

Day 1: About 20 minutes

Part 1. Pre-Teach

- Organize students in partners.

- With students, watch the video, "Amazon River" (2:33) on YouTube.

  https://youtu.be/ zSfDksLJ7l4

- Ask pairs to turn-and-talk about what they recall from watching the video about the Amazon River. You can ask questions such as: *What did you notice about the tress on the banks? How does the river change and look different? What were the flowers like?* Remind students that an inference is an unstated meaning and readers use details in the text to infer.

- Look at a map of the Amazon River and ask students what they can infer about the river.

- Read the entire poem out loud and have students follow silently and create mental pictures. Then invite students to share what the visualized.

Day 2: About 30 minutes

Part 2. Start the Shared Reading Lesson

- Give students their folders and a copy of the poem. Have students use an index card to cover up stanzas they're not reading.

- Read the title of the poem and the first two stanzas out loud. Students choral read with you.

- Ask students to volunteer to answer the following questions:

First Stanza:

> *Describe what you see.*
>
> *How do you know the Amazon is the longest river in the world?*
>
> *What do you picture when you read "Through trees that crowd the banks on either side"?*
>
> *Can you find one word to describe "the trees that crowd the banks . . . "*

Second Stanza:

> *What do you think hides in the undergrowth?*
>
> *How do you think monkeys have their fun?*
>
> *Why does the author repeat the first line of the first stanza?*

- Read Stanzas 3 and 4 out loud and have students choral read with you.

    Third Stanza:

    Why do the young men feel pride?

    Describe the picture this stanza creates in your mind and cite details that make the picture.

    Fourth Stanza:

    What are monsoons? Use information in lines three and four of this stanza to show your thinking.

- Read the last two stanzas out loud and have students choral read with you.

    Fifth Stanza:

    Why does the poet use the word "pads" for the jaguar's walk?

    Why are the jaguar's eyes bright?

    Sixth Stanza:

    Why can't one person walk the length of the Amazon?

    Why does the author end the poem by repeating two lines he has already repeated in the poem?

- Reread the poem again out loud and have students follow silently thinking about main ideas. Here are questions to help students find the main ideas—post these on chart paper for them to use:

    What are the topics?

    What details relate to each topic?

    Use details in the poem to find main ideas.

- Invite students to turn-and-talk and find one main idea.

- Pairs share with class and note two main ideas in their readers' notebooks.

Wrap Up: Notice how well students visualized, answered questions, and found main ideas.

Day 3: About 15 minutes

Part 3. Teacher Assesses

Complete the Anchor Chart

Additions and adjustments come from the students. You'll want to see what they can add. If they add little, then students might be telling you they require more practice. You can redo part of the lesson or move on and slow down, checking frequently for understanding.

- Ask students to retrieve the poem from their folders.

- Reread the poem and invite students to choral read with you.

- Reread main idea chart notes and invite students to add or adjust details.

- Review *monsoons*.

Reflect and Intervene: On sticky notes, jot the names of students who didn't participate in the shared reading lesson. Meet with them to determine whether you'll re-teach using this poem or a different poem.

Chita Rivera

The Dancer's Dancer

[1]In 1986, a 53-year-old woman was driving in New York City when she was struck by a taxi. Her leg was broken in 12 places. It took 18 screws to put the bones back together, and she was told she might never walk on that leg again. This would be terrible news for anyone. But this woman wasn't just anyone. She was one of the most famous dancers in the world.

[2]Her name at birth in 1933 was Dolores Conchita Figueroa del Rivero. Her Puerto Rican daddy, who played clarinet and saxophone in the United States Navy Band, died when she was seven. Her mother, part Scottish and part Italian, went to work to support her fatherless family. Her daughter was so full of energy she broke a coffee table leaping and dashing through the house. Her mother solved the problem by sending her to ballet classes.

[3]Learning to dance opened a new world for Dolores. With help from her brother, she put on shows in their basement. She wanted more. She took voice and piano lessons. By the time she was fifteen, Chita Rivera, as she came to be known, was so good at dancing that she tried out for the School of American Ballet in New York City. During her try out, Chita wore a painful blister on her foot, but she refused to stop dancing. When the blister broke and started bleeding, a teacher put a bandage on it, and she went right on dancing. There seemed to be no question about it. This girl had a dream, and she was never going to give up. Not only did Chita make it into the school, she won a scholarship. And two years after that, still only seventeen, she landed a role in a Broadway show, *Call Me Madam.* After touring with the show for 10 months, Chita was drawing attention. Her career was taking off.

[4]By the time of her car wreck in 1986, Rivera had been performing for 36 years. She had danced, sung, and acted her way into the hearts of millions of fans around the world. She had been <u>nominated</u> five times for Tony awards, the highest honor given for live Broadway theater. Few people had ever done more or done it better. So what now? Should she quit? Her leg was mangled. At her age, most dancers have hung up their slippers. But this was Chita Rivera. She hadn't quit as a girl. She wasn't going to quit now.

[5]In spite of the odds, she began working out, determined she would return. Slowly, painfully, her leg grew stronger until the amazing Chita Rivera was once again dancing on stage. She went on to earn five more Tony <u>nominations</u> and win two of them. She became the first Latin@ American to receive a Kennedy Center Honors award. She was awarded the Presidential Medal of Freedom. At 86: still performing, still wowing crowds, still Chita Rivera—a nation's treasure.

Lesson 22

SHARED READING OF THE SHORT TEXT, "CHITA RIVERA: THE DANCER'S DANCER"

Purpose: To determine important details to infer personality traits

Lesson Materials:

- Copies for all students of the short text, "Chita Rivera: The Dancer's Dancer"

- Students file folders for storing short texts; sheet of paper for covering paragraphs

- An anchor chart headed with the text's title. First write sentences for *nominated* and *nomination*: Our class *nominated* two students for president, but only one will win. Each student accepted the *nomination* for president, and the votes will decide who wins. Then, make two columns on the anchor chart: Title left side "Personality Traits" and right side "Text Evidence."

Video: "Chita Rivera Performs 'America' and 'All That Jazz'" (5:43) (**Note:** Only watch "America" or go to YouTube and find another introduction to Chita Rivera's dancing.)

https://youtu.be/
e2E30HG5QNs

- Video: "Broadway 101: What Is a Broadway Theatre?" (1:33) or go to YouTube and find another to build background on Broadway theater.

https://youtu.be/
9jNOwh8Qgt4

Day 1: About 20–25 minutes

Part 1. Pre-Teach

- Watch with your students the video of Chita Rivera performing "America" (only watch that performance). Invite students to turn-and-talk and discuss how they feel about Chita Rivera's performance. Students share.

- Remind students that what a person says and does reveals his or her personality traits.

- Ask students to turn-and talk about the personality traits you notice based on Chita Rivera's performance. (Students might suggest: *energetic, polished, happy, projects her enjoyment, exciting*).

- Watch with your students the video "Broadway 101: What Is a Broadway Theatre?"

- Help students understand that performing in a Broadway theater is an honor and a high point in someone's career. Also, Broadway showcases musicals such as *The Lion King* and *Aladdin* and dramas or plays that tell stories without music.

- Read the sentence on the anchor chart for *nominated* and think-aloud to show how you determine the word's meaning.

- Read aloud the sentences on the anchor chart for nomination and invite students to turn-and-talk and figure out the meaning of that word. Students share.

- Explain that *nominate* is the base word.

Day 2: About 30 minutes

Part 2. Start the Shared Reading Lesson

- Read the title and the first two paragraphs out loud and have students follow silently.

- Ask students to answer the following questions:

  What are two ways the dancer Chita Rivera could react to this accident?

  How would you describe Rivera's childhood?

  Why was Rivera a problem to her mother?

  Evaluate the way her mother solved the problem.

- Read the third paragraph out loud, have students follow silently, and then answer the questions that follow:

  What do you learn about Rivera's personality traits? Can you identify two different traits and provide support from the text?

  How do you know that Rivera's career on Broadway was taking off?

  What does this paragraph tell you about Rivera's talent?

- Read the fourth and fifth paragraphs out loud. Have students read silently and then answer the questions that follow.

  Fourth Paragraph:

  Use context to explain the meaning of nominated and nomination.

  Why are Tony Awards important to performers?

  What does Rivera's decision to not quit show about her personality?

  Fifth Paragraph:

  How did Rivera beat the odds?

  Why do you think she received a Presidential Medal of Freedom?

  Why does David Harrison call Rivera "The Dancer's Dancer?"

  Use context to explain the meaning of nominations.

Wrap Up: Notice how well students used evidence to figure out Rivera's personality traits.

Day 3: About 15–20 minutes

Part 3. Teacher Assesses

Complete the Anchor Chart

Additions and adjustments come from the students. You'll want to see what they can add. If they add little, then students might be telling you they require more practice. You can redo part of the lesson or move on and slow down, checking frequently for understanding.

- Ask students to retrieve "Chita Rivera" from their folders.

- Reread the text and invite students to choral read with you.

- Reread the chart notes and ask students to add or adjust details.

- Review *Broadway theater, nominated*, and *nominations*.

- Review meaning of *nominated* and *nominations*.

Reflect and Intervene: On sticky notes, jot the names of students who didn't participate or contribute ideas for the anchor chart. Work with individuals or a small group. Return to modeling and then invite students to respond.

Who Were They—Those First People to Walk Upon This Land?

¹Perhaps he was a jolly man
who tickled his baby,
made his young wife giggle.

²They had come a long way,
pulling their boat on shore at night
to warm themselves by a fire.
She would nurse the child
while he cut the fish he'd caught
into pieces for their dinner.

³They had left behind
their family and friends
to seek a new life.
Food at the big camp
had grown scarce.
Too many people to feed.

⁴The trip had not been easy.
Sometimes the wind
was a roaring dragon,
and the sea tried again and again
to throw them off its back.
They thought they would drown.

⁵Sometimes the frigid air
gripped them so tightly
it hurt to breathe.
Sometimes they went days without food.
Then the mother's milk was not enough
to keep the starving baby from crying.

⁶Not knowing they had done it,
one day they paddled past
the end of one place
to the beginning of another.

⁷When they came ashore,
their feet left prints in the soft sand—
his and hers—
the first human prints in a new world
that fifteen thousand years later
would be called
North America.

Lesson 23

SHARED READING OF THE POEM, "WHO WERE THEY—THOSE FIRST PEOPLE TO WALK UPON THIS LAND?"

Purpose: To use details to visualize, make inferences, and determine main ideas

Lesson Materials:

- Copies for all students of the poem, "Who Were They—Those First People to Walk Upon This Land?"

- Students' file folders for storing short texts; 4 × 6 index card for covering stanzas

- An anchor chart headed with the title of the poem. Make two columns on the chart: Title left side "Drawing Conclusions," and halfway down write, "Main Ideas." Title right side "Text Evidence."

https://youtu.be/jaizoayO9yU

- Video: "Peopling the Americas" (9:16), or go to YouTube and find another.

Day 1: About 20–25 minutes

Part 1. Pre-Teach

- Watch the YouTube video with students: "Peopling the Americas." Discuss with students: *What are the two theories of how the Paleo-Indians came to North America? Where did these people come from? Did they have cities? What were their cities like? How did they get food? Who really discovered America?*

- Assess what students know about inferring, finding main ideas, and visualizing. Explain that the details in the poem will help them infer or find unstated meanings about the people and their new homes.

- Have partners use the guidelines to discuss main ideas. Find one to two main ideas in the poem by doing the following:

Select details.

Use the details to figure out the general topic.

What is most important about the topic?

Write that as your main idea.

- Remind students that specific details also support painting a mental picture.

- Model making inferences using the first stanza. Phrases such as "jolly man, tickled baby, young wife giggle" help me infer that the first people coming to America were like you and me—they were happy, enjoyed family, and laughed.

- Read the entire poem out loud and have students follow silently.

Day 2: About 30 minutes

Part 2. Start the Shared Reading Lesson

- Read the title and first three stanzas out loud. Students follow silently and use their index card to cover up the rest of the poem.

- Have students think about each question/prompt and volunteer to answer. Questions begin with second and third stanzas.

Second and Third Stanzas:

Use the details to conclude how the family of three felt on their first night on land.

Why did people leave family and friends to make this journey?

Explain the meaning of "scarce" using clues in the stanza.

Why was food scarce?

Fourth Stanza:

Why does the author compare the wind to a roaring dragon?

What do you picture when you read comparison (metaphor)?

Explain why people thought they might drown.

Fifth Stanza:

Explain the meaning of frigid and use details to help you.

Why was it hard for them to breathe at times?

Use the details in this stanza to draw conclusions about what life was like.

Sixth and Seventh Stanzas:

Why does the author stay, "Not knowing they had done it . . . ?"

Turn-and-talk to a classmate; use details in the poem to find one main idea. Share with the class, making sure you offer details to support your thinking.

Choose a stanza and create a mental picture. Use words to describe what you see and volunteer to share.

Day 3: About 20 minutes

Wrap Up: Notice how well students drew conclusions, developed mental pictures, and identified main ideas.

Part 3. Teacher Assesses

Complete the Anchor Chart

Additions and adjustments come from the students. You'll want to see what they can add. If they add little, then students might be telling you they require more practice. You can redo part of the lesson or move on and slow down, checking frequently for understanding.

- Ask students to retrieve the poem from their folders.

- Reread the poem and invite students to choral read with you.

- Reread the chart notes and invite students to add or adjust details.

Reflect and Intervene: On sticky notes, jot the names of students who didn't participate or contribute ideas for the anchor chart. Work with individuals or a small group. Return to modeling and then invite students to respond.

Solving an Ancient Cave Mystery

Note: *This is the story of Riverbluff Cave, which was discovered in Springfield, Missouri, on 9/11 (September 11, 2001). David's book about how the cave was found and explored is called* Cave Detectives, Unraveling the Mysteries of an Ice Age Cave.

[1]On September 11, 2001, men building a road in Springfield, Missouri, used dynamite to blast a limestone outcropping out of their way. When the dust settled, the men found themselves staring down a hole in the ceiling of a cave. Holding up a cigarette lighter, one man crept a few steps into the darkness. At the edge of a steep drop-off, he stopped. In the poor light, he couldn't see the bottom. He turned around and got out of there.

[2]A scientist was called in to look around. On a wall above his head, he spotted huge claw marks gouged into the clay, 14 feet above the floor—four feet higher than a basketball goal. He knew at once what beast made those marks—a short-faced bear, the largest bear that ever lived. The giant creature was five, maybe six feet tall, could weigh more than half a ton, and run 30 or 40 miles an hour. But short-faced bears became extinct more than 10,000 years ago! This was a major discovery! What other secrets might lie hidden down that dark hall?

[3]The scientist chose a team and set out to explore the cave. Always walking carefully, they returned again and again. Again and again they were amazed. Round areas scooped in the thick red clay showed where bears had their cubs. Claw marks were left by two other extinct hunters: the American lion and saber-tooth cat. How did these creatures get in?

[4]Trip after trip, the team pressed on, sometimes crawling in tight places. At last, in a spot where ceiling met floor, they found where a stream once entered through a small opening. Over time, the entrance filled up with debris and sealed the cave forever. One mystery solved.

[5]A few hundred feet from there was a deep pit, its walls crisscrossed by bear claws. Not far away were thousands of tracks left in the clay by animals with sharp hooves. And stuck in the mud was the clue that solved the puzzle. It was part of the foot of a peccary—a distant cousin of the pig. Tooth marks showed where something had gnawed the foot from the body.

[6]Pieces of the picture fell into place. Long ago, a short-face bear walking along the stream entered the cave. Moving carefully, it made its way through the darkness to the pit. Sometime later, a band of peccaries sniffed at the opening. Maybe they'd been there before. Maybe they milled around before their leader went in. The rest followed down the black hall, unaware of their looming fate. Suddenly, the bear roared up from below and grabbed a terrified peccary by the foot. Squealing peccaries scattered in panic. All but one. Soon, the only sound in the cave was the bear, working its terrible jaws.

[7]Ancient mystery solved. How ancient? When the scientist had tests run, he was in for a shock. The bear ate the peccary more than 55,000 years ago.

Lesson 24

SHARED READING OF THE SHORT TEXT, "SOLVING AN ANCIENT CAVE MYSTERY"

Purpose: To practice cause/effect; to determine main ideas; to understand how scientists used evidence to solve the mystery

Lesson Materials:

- Copies for all students of the short text, "Solving an Ancient Cave Mystery"

- Students' file folders for storing short texts; a blank sheet of paper to cover up paragraphs

- An anchor chart headed with the title of the text. Write the sentences for *gouged*, *extinct*, and *debris* on the chart: The squirrel *gouged* a hole in the yard and buried a walnut. Short-faced bears no longer roam the earth because they are *extinct*. Debris like twigs, rocks, rusty cans, and dirt closed the gophers' holes in the meadow.

- Make two columns on the anchor chart under the sentences. Title left side "Cause" and right side "Effects." Use the bottom or back of the chart to note main ideas.

- Video: "What is an Ice Age?" (2:08), or find another video on YouTube.

  https://youtu.be/ dJ5GYQrkvxI

- Invite students to share what they learned about the Ice Age.

- Find a map of Missouri online and show students where Springfield is. You might share that the author of the story, David Harrison, lives in Springfield, MO.

- Explain that the video they'll watch next is about the Riverbluff Cave that formed during an Ice Age.

  https://youtu.be/ J50KJ7304ps

- Video: "Ice Age Cave" (4:21)

Day 1: About 20 minutes

Part 1. Pre-Teach

- Watch with students the YouTube video: "What is an Ice Age?" (Note: You might have to watch each video twice so students recall more details.)

- Have students turn-and-talk about what they learned from "What is an Ice Age?" and share responses with classmates.

- Organize students into pairs and have them discuss these questions: *What are some animals found in the cave? How did the scientist know the claw tracks were made by a short-faced bear? Why was this a major discovery? How do scientists believe other animals entered the cave? Describe what you picture when the author writes: "Soon the only sound in the cave was the bear, working its terrible jaws." Do you think the cave will be a tourist attraction? Explain.*

- Locate Springfield, Missouri, on a map and discuss its location in relation to where you and your students live.

- Read the sentences on the anchor chart, one at a time, for these words: *gouged*, *extinct*, and *debris*. Think aloud and model how you figure out the meaning of *gouged*. Invite students to use context clues to determine the meaning of *extinct* and *debris*.

- Review cause/effect with students. Explain that a cause can be an event, words spoken, weather, and so forth. The effect(s) are things that happen as a result of the cause.

Day 2: About 30 minutes

Part 2. Start the Shared Reading Lesson

- Reread the title and the first two paragraphs out loud. Students follow silently and cover up paragraphs not being read with blank sheet of paper.

- Ask students to discuss the following questions:

  Why was finding the cave an accident?

  Why did the man stop exploring the cave?

  What animal found in the cave is extinct?

  How does the short-faced bear differ from bears today?

  If the cause is, "A scientist was called to look around?" what are the effects?

- Reread the third and fourth paragraphs out loud and have students follow silently and then answer the questions that follow.

  In the third paragraph, if the cause is, "Men returned again and again to the cave," list the effects.

  Why was it difficult to find the cave's entrance?

  What other extinct animals lived in the cave?

- Reread the fifth paragraph to the end out loud and have students follow silently and then answer the questions that follow.

  What is a peccary?

  Can you predict what animal gnawed the foot? What details helped you make the prediction?

- Reread the sixth paragraph and create a *cause statement* plus the resulting *effects*.

- Find one to two main ideas using this process:

  Select details.

  Use the details to figure out the general topic.

  What is most important about the topic?

  Share your main idea.

Wrap Up: Notice how students use context to determine the meaning of words, how well they identified cause and effect and found main ideas.

Part 3. Teacher Assesses

Complete the Anchor Chart

Additions and adjustments come from the students. You'll want to see what they can add. If they add little, then students might be telling you they require more practice. You can redo part of the lesson or move on and slow down, checking frequently for understanding.

- Ask students to retrieve the text from their folders.

- Reread the text and invite students to choral read with you.

- Reread the chart notes and invite students to add or adjust details.

- Review *gouged, extinct,* and *debris*; introduce *extinction.*

Reflect and Intervene: On sticky notes, jot the names of students who didn't participate or contribute ideas for the anchor chart. Work with individuals or a small group. Return to modeling and then invite students to respond.

Next Steps for Guided Practice and Growth in Reading

In my more than 45 years of teaching, I have never met a child who didn't want to learn to read well. At school, being able to read means participating in book clubs, student- and teacher-led discussions, working as a team with peers on a project, sharing book talks on podcasts, completing independent reading, and notebook writing about reading. This is one aspect of equity—going to school every day and having the reading skill to be able to be a full participant in every class.

David Harrison's poems and stories are not only accessible to dependent readers, but they also introduce learners to the sounds and rhythms of words and poetic language. Rich images, similes, and metaphors foster visualization, and research points out that what we can imagine and picture we understand and can write about (De Koning & van der Schoot, 2013; Lian & Galda, 2010; Self, 1987). In addition, having a poetic soul has enabled Harrison to bring rich imagery and detailed descriptions to the short texts, supporting students' visualizing to improve comprehension and recall.

Once students have completed the lessons, they can choose a piece for practice and performance to improve fluency and comprehension (Rasinski & Griffith, 2011).

Independent reading happens every day because it boosts reading skill.

You can also add texts to their folders by including the poems and short texts in the appendix.

FIGURE 5.1: THREE FOURTH GRADERS IN JENNIFER HARRISON'S CLASS HAVE FUN READING "THE AMAZON RAIN FOREST."

IMPROVE FLUENCY: PRACTICE AND PERFORMANCE USING GUIDED PRACTICE TEXTS

Seventh grader Helena Hustick reflects practicing and performing poetry in fifth grade. *"In fifth grade, I think practicing and performing poetry gave me more confidence in reading. I loved choosing a poem and working with a partner. Now, I read poetry a lot. I think the practice got me into it [reading poems]."*

These words from Helena reveal the powerful influence practicing and performing poems can have on developing readers. Once you and students have completed guided practice, set aside time for students to practice and perform the poems or a part of a short text.

According to Rasinski and Griffith (2011), being a fluent reader is critical to students being able to learn to read. They recommend repeated practice, and that's what students gain when you consistently involve them in a weekly routine for at least one semester, preferably more if time permits. Here are some guidelines to help with repeated practice:

- **Students choose.** Organize students into practice partners and invite partners to decide whether they'll choose a poem or short text. Pairs should select different pieces—this can be two poems, two short texts, or a poem and short text. (Note: Students select two to three consecutive paragraphs from a short text and check these. The entire poem should be read.) Have students date their pieces once they've selected one. Poems and short texts remain in folders. Students place their dated selection at the top of the pieces for easy access.

- **Students practice using a weekly routine.** On the first day of practice, usually a Monday, pairs take turns reading their piece out loud. They also discuss how the poem makes them feel and what it means to them. Remind students to pause and take a breath after commas, dashes, and periods; invite partners to help each other. Circulate among pairs as they practice reading noticing expressive reading, offering a tip, and answering any questions students might have. Set aside about four to five minutes each day for practice.

- **Students perform once each week.** On Friday, students perform their poem or short text in front of the class. If a student resists performance, don't insist. Instead, have conversations with the student to explore the resistance, and then as he or she practices, notice all the positives in their reading.

- **Students set expectations for performance.** I recommend you have students set up a few expectations for performing and have the class set expectations for listening and noticing what peers did well.

You can revisit and adjust these after four to five weeks. Have students set up expectations, and adjust them, if necessary, after several practices. Many students will be nervous and may be inaudible and/or race through the poem to get the experience behind them. This is fine and to be expected. Be positive and remind them to slow down before the next practice. The chart below shows the expectations set by the students, both for performers and for their audience.

Performance Expectations for Students

- Read with expression and loud enough for others to hear.

- Hold paper below your face so you can be heard.

- Take a breath at punctuation.

Expectations for the Audience

- Listen.

- Be positive when you notice something about the performance.

To support students learning how to respond to a performance, teachers and I did the noticing and questioning for about five to six weeks. With the class, we established what to notice: read with expression; spoke clearly; made eye contact with audience; enjoyed reading the poem; stopped at punctuation; liked the poem because it was funny (or another reason).

- **Bring in other texts.** If you'd like to extend the practice and performance, then I suggest you use multicultural poems and readers' theater scripts. Ask your school's media specialist for help, if you have one; otherwise, seek help from the children's librarian in your public library or search on the Internet. I've listed dozens of books in Appendix J. Based on Dr. Rasinski's work at the Kent State University's reading clinic, extending students' practice and performance of poetry and readers' theater to a second semester or the entire school year can have positive effects on students' reading comprehension.

BENEFITS TO STUDENTS OF PRACTICE AND PERFORMANCE

Through practice and performance, students begin to see themselves as readers who can improve expression, fluency, vocabulary, comprehension, and at the same time, have fun and develop self-confidence. In the book *Fluency Through Practice & Performance* (2011), Rasinski, who directs the Kent State Reading Clinic, points out that most developing readers who spend a month at the clinic can make more than a month's progress in reading. Lorraine Griffith, a fifth-grade teacher, and Chase Young, a second-grade teacher, are two among many teachers whose students show gains of up to 2.9 years growth in their students' reading achievement (Rasinski & Griffith, 2011, p. 139). Though not scientifically based, practice and performance with other learning practices can improve students' reading. Rasinski and Griffith call for teachers to move reading instruction away from only using scientific research to including the artistic and aesthetic value of reading.

TRANSFER LEARNING FROM GUIDED PRACTICE TO INSTRUCTIONAL AND INDEPENDENT READING

Transferring learning to other situations asks students to take what they learned and practiced during guided practice lessons and transfer strategies and skills to instructional and independent reading. For example, when you can dance classical ballet and then learn to do modern dance or when you drive a tractor and then learn to drive a car, transfer occurs.

If dependent readers gain confidence and skill during guided practice in applying strategies such as inferring, visualizing, compare/contrast, cause/effect, finding themes, understanding literary elements, and so forth, transfer means these students can apply practiced strategies to longer instructional texts as well as to their independent reading. The big question is, What can you do to foster transfer? One sure point is that transfer doesn't happen automatically with developing readers, and the guided practice lessons are the "we do" part of the gradual release model that eventually moves students to "you do." Here are some teaching tips that provide a pathway to transfer for your students.

- **Review the strategy.** Refresh students' memory of what they practiced during a lesson that featured the strategy you want them to transfer to other material.

- **Have students explain the strategy.** Ask students to tell you everything they remember about the strategy: how it helps readers, what to do to apply it to a text, questions they have.

- **Provide a mental model.** Listen carefully to students' explanations and frame your think-aloud and lesson so that it supports students' questions and any gaps in their knowledge that you noticed. Remember, what students can visualize is a solid measure of what they understand.

- **Practice as a small group.** Pull small groups that require additional practice and support them. You can use the text students practiced with or a different text (see Appendix I for additional texts). You can skip supporting a small group if students recall enough to move directly to partner work.

- **Partner students.** Pair students and explain they will practice the strategy with their partner. Circulate and listen to students' talk providing support when necessary.

- **Invite students to work independently.** Using the gradual release model, invite students to work independently using a small section of an instructional text they'll be reading. I recommend that you also ask students to complete notebook writing that can show you their level of understanding and transfer. You can use one of your cold writing pieces as a model for students.

- **Determine your next teaching moves.** Students will need to practice transferring strategies to other texts until most of the group or class can do it. The time frame will differ. The point is to set aside enough practice time so students transfer the strategy. Your goal will always try to move students to independence through scaffolding and, when necessary, re-teaching.

TEACHING AND LEARNING REMINDER

I'm closing with an important reminder: There are three instructional pieces that are game changers for students. The first is the instructional read-aloud where students can see you, the expert, thinking about and responding to books. The second is students' self-selecting books for independent reading. For students to transfer independent reading from school to home, you'll need to set aside time for them to read at school. The third is offering students guided practice with the lessons in this book and by developing your own. This type of practice can move developing readers forward in the 10 ways that follow:

1) **Personal efficacy and power of YET:** As students improve, they build their

personal efficacy and apply Carol Dweck's power of YET to daily learning experiences. The power of YET (Dweck, 2007) helps students realize that their successes grow out of daily practice and teacher support. With time, hard work, and support, they come to understand that it's possible to reach goals; "I can't do it" becomes "I can't do it *yet*." I invite teachers to discuss both terms with students as well as create and display an anchor chart that celebrates progress through the power of YET.

2) **Ability to talk about their reading:** By observing their teacher talk about books and practicing with a partner, students develop the skill to communicate their thoughts and ideas to others. Talking about reading is a complex process that asks students to develop ideas and clarify them so others understand their thinking.

3) **Sense of community:** As students collaborate with each other and their teacher, they develop the relationships and support network that continually builds a community of learners. Teamwork increases trust and empathy through students' shared discussions about books and projects, and trust and empathy are like the mortar between bricks, bonding members to one another.

4) **Reflection and self-evaluation:** Students reflect during the lessons when they turn-and-talk to a partner, refine and adjust their hunches, and jot thoughts in their notebooks. During conferences with their teacher, students can review several weeks of notebook writing or specific entries to self-evaluate their progress with reading and growth in writing about reading.

5) **Use of text details to think:** Recalling facts and details is a basic aspect of comprehension. Shared reading nudges students to use details and facts to infer, connect ideas within a text, determine important information, and support diverse interpretations.

6) **Reading fluency:** During each shared reading lesson, students hear their teacher's fluent reading of texts as they follow and read silently. When students reread short texts they have stored in a folder and/or choose a poem to practice and perform, they can develop fluent, expressive reading that reflects their comprehension and interpretation.

7) **Listening skills:** When students talk about reading during pair-shares, small group discussions, and conferences with teachers, they learn to focus, listen, and remember.

8) **Word knowledge:** During lessons, students will practice using context to figure out a word's meaning; they'll also observe their teacher doing this during interactive read-alouds. Over time, the skill of using context clues to figure out a word's meaning will be a strategy that students can use with ease.

9) **Background knowledge:** All lessons build students' background knowledge by having them watch, listen to, and discuss recommended videos. In addition, you'll introduce vocabulary that students need to comprehend the text. Having prior knowledge increases students' understanding and enjoyment of their reading.

10) **Self-confidence**: As students' reading skill improves, so does their self-confidence and willingness to continue to choose to read self-selected books at school and home.

TIME TO REFLECT

Reserve time to mull over what you've read in this chapter. Discuss the questions that follow with yourself or a colleague who is also reading this book.

- How does practice and performance of poems and short texts benefit students?
- Why is transfer important to learning?
- Why should you make time for independent reading in your class?

APPENDIX A

Suggested ELA Schedule for 45 Minutes

These times are estimates. No doubt, some lessons will take more time—some less time. Make adjustments as needed. The two elements that, if possible, should remain constant are independent reading of self-selected books and the three guided practice lessons. In addition, guided practice lessons work best if they are on consecutive days.

POSSIBLE SCHEDULE FOR 45-MINUTE ELA CLASS INCLUDING GUIDED PRACTICE

Monday	Tuesday	Wednesday	Thursday	Friday
Independent reading: 15 minutes	Independent reading: 15 minutes	Independent reading: 15 minutes	Independent reading: 15 minutes	Independent reading: 15 minutes
Interactive teacher read-aloud: 12 minutes	Interactive teacher read-aloud: 12 minutes	Guided practice: 20 minutes	Guided practice: 20 minutes	Guided practice: 20 minutes
Instructional reading: 15 minutes	Instructional reading: 15 minutes	Teacher confers: 8 minutes; students read or do notebook work	Teacher confers: 8 minutes; students read or do notebook work	Teacher confers: 8 minutes; students read or do notebook work
Wrap up	Wrap up	Wrap up	Wrap up	Wrap up

APPENDIX B

Suggested ELA Schedule for 60 Minutes

Since there is more flexibility with the 60-minute ELA schedule, teachers will have time to confer and pull small groups to discuss reading. They could also add practicing and performing poetry for an entire semester (see pages 118–120).

POSSIBLE SCHEDULE FOR 60-MINUTE ELA CLASS INCLUDING GUIDED PRACTICE

Monday	Tuesday	Wednesday	Thursday	Friday
Independent reading: 15 minutes	Independent reading: 15 minutes	Independent reading: 20 minutes	Independent reading: 15 minutes	Independent reading: 20 minutes
Interactive teacher read-aloud: 15 minutes	Interactive teacher read-aloud: 15 minutes	Interactive teacher read-aloud: 15 minutes	Confer/ small groups, notebook writing: 14 minutes	Interactive teacher read-aloud: 17 minutes
Instructional reading, confer, small groups, notebook writing: 28 minutes	Instructional reading, confer, small groups, notebook writing: 28 minutes	Guided practice: 20 minutes	Guided practice: 30 minutes	Guided practice: 20 minutes
Wrap up	Wrap up	Wrap up	Wrap up	Wrap up

APPENDIX C
Literary Elements Handout for Students

It's easy to turn literary elements into prompts and questions to discuss fictional texts. You can introduce literary elements using the interactive read-aloud, and students can practice with narrative texts.

Antagonists: Forces that work against the protagonist and create tension in narrative texts. There are two kinds of antagonists:

External: nature, other characters, decisions, actions taken, interactions

Internal: thoughts within the character's mind and emotions

Climax: The moment or point of greatest intensity in the plot. Short stories usually have one climax, but novels can have small climaxes as the plot unfolds. The major climax is near the end. The climax, the highest point of the action, can deepen comprehension of plot details and also offer insights into themes.

Conflicts: Struggles or differences between opposing forces such as the protagonist and nature, two characters, the protagonist and a specific event or situation, or an internal conflict within the character. Some conflicts become problems. For example, the inner conflict of deciding whether to drive in a snowstorm leads to a problem when the person's car becomes stuck in a snowdrift on a desolate road. Observing how characters deal with inner conflicts and conflicts with other characters and/or a setting can reveal much about their personalities and the themes of the narrative.

Denouement or Return to Normalcy: Events that resolve the climax in a novel, short story, drama, or narrative poem are often referred to as the outcome. Understanding outcomes of a narrative can lead to figuring out themes and central themes and deepen readers' understanding of how the plot brought them back to a feeling of normalcy.

Other Characters: Observing how other characters relate to, dialogue, and interact with the protagonist can deepen readers' knowledge of all their personalities as well as the themes in a story.

Plot: Events that occur in a text and enable readers to observe characters in diverse situations. Plot supports an understanding of theme, conflicts, setting, and characters' personalities. Often referred to as rising action, the plot in a text builds from the opening of the story to a high point of interest called the climax.

Point of View: This refers to who's narrating the story.

- A first person narrator is often the protagonist, and the author uses first person pronouns: I, me, mine, we, us, our, ours.
- An objective narrator acts like an observer who sees and records information and events from a neutral perspective and uses third person pronouns: he, him, his, she, her, hers, it, its, they, them, their, theirs.

- An omniscient narrator knows everything about the characters, their conflicts and problems, decisions and motivation, thoughts and feelings. Told from the third person point of view, it uses these pronouns: he, him, his, she, her, hers, it, its, they, them, their, theirs.

Protagonist: The main character in the narrative who has problems to solve. Observing how the protagonist interacts with others, makes decisions, and tries to solve problems offers insight into this character's personality and motivations.

Problem: Something that gets in the way of a character's desire or goal and requires an action or decision to overcome, such as whether to risk diving from the high board as required by the PE teacher when you're a weak swimmer or lying to your parents about where you've been to avoid punishment. Problems require characters to figure out solutions such as having no money for food or coping after a hurricane's wind and rain destroyed part of their town. How characters tackle problems and deal with their inability to resolve some can provide readers with deep insights into personality and decision-making processes.

Setting: The time and place of the narrative. A short text can focus on one setting while longer texts have multiple settings. How characters function in and react to a setting can deepen readers' understanding of characters' motivation and personality traits.

Symbolism: A symbol is one thing that represents an idea, emotion, or concept. For example, the U.S. flag symbolizes patriotism and love of country; white symbolizes purity; and red symbolizes blood or love. Narrative authors sometimes select objects to symbolize or represent an emotion or idea they're trying to help the reader understand.

Theme: This is a statement about people and life that the author makes with the narrative. In folktales and fairy tales, theme is frequently stated as a moral or lesson at the end of the story.

 Available for download at resources.corwin.com/guidedpractice

APPENDIX D

Self-Evaluation Questions/Prompts for Students

Directions

1. Ask students to head a page in their notebooks or use a separate piece of paper: include name, date, and the title of the poem(s) or short text(s) they're referencing.

2. Have students jot a few notes about the question and then use their notes to write a few sentences.

3. Start by inviting students to answer one question/prompt. Then, add a second if you feel students can tackle two.

Write about your discussions by answering these questions/prompts.

Write the questions you discussed. Are you using details from the text to support your thinking? Give an example from your partner discussion.

Review your notebook and answer these questions.

Are you jotting notes before you write? Give an example. How do these notes help with the writing? Are your entries getting longer and more detailed? Are you including text evidence? Give an example to show this.

Use context clues in the text to figure out the meaning of a word.

Give an example from the text of how context clues helped you figure out a word's meaning. Explain why using context clues can improve your reading and understanding.

New information you've learned.

List the new information you learned from the video you watched and from the selection. *Then answer*: How does having this information help you better understand the poem or text?

 Available for download at resources.corwin.com/guidedpractice

APPENDIX E: COMPARE/CONTRAST HANDOUT FOR STUDENTS

Students can use the Venn diagram to jot notes to show likeness where the circles overlap and write differences on the right and left of the overlap. Or you can ask students to list likeness in their notebooks and then divide the rest of the page in half lengthwise and note differences on the left and right sides.

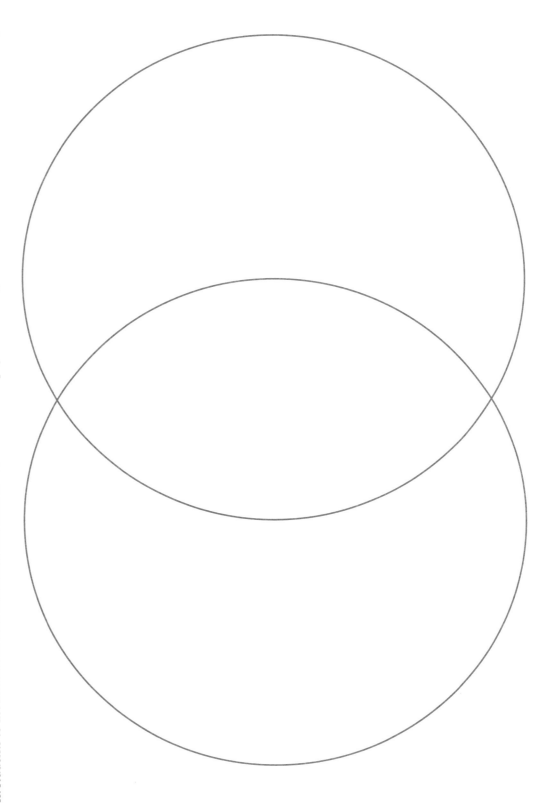

APPENDIX F
Guidelines for Planning a Shared Reading Lesson

The shared reading lessons in this book have been carefully preplanned before writing each one. Remember, these lessons use an anchor chart to introduce vocabulary and note students' thinking as they apply a reading strategy and answer questions. You'll want to develop shared reading lessons using some of David Harrison's texts in Appendix I as well as identifying texts you believe your students can learn from and enjoy. These can be a chapter from a novel, a short story, a fairy tale or folktale, myth, article from a magazine' or an excerpt from an informational chapter book.

On Appendix H, you'll find a list of magazines that have short texts you can use.

For shared reading lessons to meet students' needs, it's important to carefully think each lesson through and to use the questions that follow in the preplanning process.

Questions for Preplanning Shared Reading Lessons

- Will the text interest students?

- Can students, with support, read the text?

- What vocabulary should I introduce? How will I introduce these words? Present three to four new words and the forms of each word for the lesson.

- Do students need to build background knowledge and vocabulary by watching a short video or looking at a series of photographs?

- Will I have students' complete notebook writing about vocabulary and/or background knowledge?

- How will I chunk the text or divide it into parts?

- How am I ensuring that students do most of the work?

- Have I prepared an anchor chart with vocabulary and questions?

- Do I need to read the entire text aloud first and ask students to follow silently?

- Will students work with a partner or independently?

- Will I ask students to choral read with me, read silently, or read aloud with a partner by sharing the text?

- How will I know students understood and learned from the lesson?

- What are my next steps?

APPENDIX G

Guidelines for Preplanning a Partner Discussions Lesson

Similar to shared reading lessons, partner discussion lessons also increase students' vocabulary and enlarge their background knowledge. However, writing about reading is an integral part of these lessons, and teachers cold write for students to provide a resource and build their mental model of the process. In addition, students always work with a partner during vocabulary work, while building background knowledge and using prompts to discuss the text and offer text evidence as support.

You'll want to develop partner discussion lessons using some of David Harrison's texts found in Appendix I as well as identify texts you believe your students can learn from and enjoy. These can be a chapter from a novel, a short story, fairy tale or folktale, myth, article from a magazine, or an excerpt from an informational chapter book. In Appendix H, you'll find a list of magazines that have short texts you can use. Use the questions in the preplanning process that follow to develop lessons:

Questions for Preplanning Partner Discussion Lessons

- Will the text interest students?

- Can students, with support, read the text?

- What vocabulary should I introduce? How will I introduce these words? Present three to four new words and their forms for the lesson.

- Am I introducing other forms of each word?

- Do students need to build background knowledge and vocabulary by watching a short video or looking at a series of photographs?

- How will I chunk the text or divide it into parts?

- Have I thought through the cold writing I'll present in my teacher's notebook?

- Am I offering students choice in selecting a topic to write about in their readers' notebooks?

- Am I using students' notebook writing for formative assessments?

APPENDIX H

Magazine Resources for Short Texts for Guided Practice Lessons

The first five magazines listed below are from Scholastic: classroommagazines.scholastic.com/all-magazines.html

1. *Storyworks*
2. *Action*
3. *Junior Scholastic*
4. *Super Science*
5. *Science World*
6. *Zoobooks*: https://shop.zoobooks.com/
7. *Cricket*: cricketmedia.com
8. *Time for Kids*: timeforkids.com
9. *Sport Illustrated Kids*: sikids.com
10. *Faces*: cricketmedia.com
11. *Cobblestone*: cricketmedia.com
12. *OWL*: owlkids.com
13. *Dig Into History:* cricketmedia.com/dig
14. *Youth Runner*: youthrunner.com

APPENDIX I

Additional Short Texts and Poems by David L. Harrison

David L. Harrison wrote the two short texts and two poems on the following pages for you and your students! We both hope that having these texts at your fingertips will be helpful as you plan your own guided practice lessons.

- **Short Greek Myth for Guided Practice**: "**And Zeus Said (Maybe) . . .**"
- **Short Informational Text for Guided Practice**: "**Going . . . Going . . . Gone?**"
- **Poem for Guided Practice**: "**Wanting to Be Needed**"
- **Poem for Guided Practice**: "**The Last Northern White Rhinoceros**"

Short Greek Myth for Guided Practice
And Zeus Said (Maybe) . . .

"Let there be games in my honor!" Zeus might have thundered from his palace in the clouds above Mt. Olympus, back in 776 BC. He was king of all the gods so he could have anything he wanted. It was a big family and everybody had a job. Zeus's wife, Hera, was in charge of women, marriage, and family. His moody brother, Poseidon, ruled the ocean. Get him riled up, he could cause storms and make the whole earth shake. His older brother, Hades, was in charge of the underworld. Enough said about him. There was a god of love, a god of agriculture, a god of metalwork, a god of arts and music—you name it, the ancient Greeks had a god for it.

But the head god—the king over everybody—was Zeus. He was god of sky and weather and was said to throw bolts of lightning when he was upset. Mess with him, he might turn you into a constellation of stars and hang you in the night sky forever. So if he wanted to have games in his honor, why not?

All we know is that about 2,800 years ago *someone* got the idea of starting games in honor of Zeus. The early games weren't as big as the ones we have today. They were mostly running, wrestling, fighting, javelin throwing, and racing horses and chariots. They were held on Mt. Olympus, the highest point in Greece, in a large, quiet area called a sanctuary, which was dedicated to Zeus. Athletes came from all parts of the Greek empire, hoping to win honor for their cities. Winners were rewarded with a crown woven from olive leaves that were thought to be sacred. Only men and boys could compete, and only males and unmarried women could come to watch. Married women were strictly forbidden. A married woman who sneaked in and got caught could be put to death. Besides, women had their own Olympic races anyway.

The Olympics began as a festival to honor Zeus, and religion was still an important part of it for much of the next one thousand years. Crowds of 40,000 or more came to watch and take part in the festival, which was held every four years.

Today we have Summer Olympics and Winter Olympics, and they are each held every four years so that they happen two years apart. Together they include about 40 sports in hundreds of events. More than 14,000 athletes from 200 nations come to compete as more than three billion people sit by their TVs and watch from around the world.

That old Greek god Zeus would be proud to know what has happened to the event that started in his honor. Best of all, he never had to throw a single lightning bolt to get his way.

 Available for download at resources.corwin.com/guidedpractice

Short Informational Text for Guided Practice

Going . . . Going . . . Gone?

About 4.5 billion years ago when Earth was created from a spinning cloud of gas and dust, other planets formed, too, as our solar system came together. At first, Earth was little more than a large, fiery rock with a boiling surface hurling through space around the sun. It didn't have an atmosphere like we have today to protect it from the sun's burning rays or keep rocks from space from slamming into its surface. One rock was so big it broke off a chunk of Earth and sent it flying 238,900 miles away to form our moon.

After a billion years or so Earth settled down enough for its surface to cool into an outer crust (where we live), a good atmosphere to form, and enough rain to fall to make the oceans. The first signs of life appeared. In the 3.5 billion years since then, an amazing variety of plants and animals have lived on our planet. Scientists don't know how many there are because we find new ones every year, and many die off before we learn about them. We know only a small percent of all the plants and animals there are, maybe 14 out of every 100. A recent *best guess* by scientists is that there could be 298,000 kinds of plants and 8.7 million kinds of animals on Earth. We have studied only 1.2 million kinds of animals.

For plants and animals to die (become extinct) is normal. Every year around the world, thousands of species disappear. New species may come along, but it takes a very long time to happen. Some scientists think as many as nine out of 10 animals that have ever lived are now extinct. Since life began on Earth, there have been five periods when huge numbers of plants and animals died off, far more than usual. They were all caused by nature. Gigantic volcano eruptions created monster earthquakes, spread fires, made water youthrunner.com unfit to drink, and cooled the air by partly blocking sunlight with clouds of dust. The most recent mass die-off was 65 million years ago. A huge object from space blasted into the planet so hard it choked the air with dust and made temperatures drop. Many kinds of plants and animals, including the mighty dinosaurs, soon disappeared forever.

Today we're in the sixth period when plants and animals are perishing faster than normal. But this one isn't caused by nature. It's not because of volcanoes or earthquakes or meteors from space. It's being caused by us. Human activities are warming the atmosphere. Glaciers are melting. Ocean levels are rising. Weather is changing. We are polluting air and water; destroying coral reefs; killing animals for their ivory or hides; plowing under, concreting over, and poisoning plants that animals must have for food. Today human activities are quickly undoing what it took 3.5 billion years to create—a balance in nature among all the plants and animals who were sharing the planet before humans came along.

 Available for download at resources.corwin.com/guidedpractice

Poem for Guided Practice

Wanting to Be Needed

She sits beside the wheelchair
like any other dog—
waiting for a pat or a treat—
but she is not any other dog.

Head up, eyes bright,
aware of everything
that moves or makes a sound around
the girl in the chair,
she knows things other dogs don't,
can do things other dogs can't—
pull the wheelchair,
pick up dropped items,
turn on lights,
calm her mistress when she's upset.

This is her life,
what she lives for,
what she is trained to do.
Head up, eyes bright,
she sits beside the wheelchair,
wanting to be needed.

 Available for download at resources.corwin.com/guidedpractice

Poem for Guided Practice

The Last Northern White Rhinoceros

No longer bold
as rhinos go,
weakened, slow,
sick, old.

Didn't know
his kind had passed,
he was the last
male white rhino.

Fate was cast.
One by one.
Poacher's gun.
Blast by blast.

Nowhere to run.
Ancient breed.
Human's need.
Greed won.

Senseless deed.
Butchers' scorn.
Last male born.
Too late to heed.

Tired, worn,
future denied,
the last male died.
Who's to mourn?

 Available for download at resources.corwin.com/guidedpractice

APPENDIX J

Books and Poetry for Instructional and Independent Reading

STEP INTO READING SERIES (PENGUIN RANDOM HOUSE)

Bones, Level 2 by Stephen Krensky

Penguins, Level 2 by David Salomon

The Statue of Liberty, Level 2 by Lucille Recht Penner

Wild Sea Creatures: Sharks, Whales, and Dolphins! Level 2 By Chris Kratt and Martin Kratt

Dolphins! Level 3 by Sharon Bokoske

Hungry, Hungry Sharks, Level 3 by Joanna Cole

Michelle Obama, Level 3 by Shana Corey

Monster Bugs, Level 3 by Lucille Recht Penner

S-S-Snakes! Level 3 by Lucille Recht Penner

Space: Planets, Moons, Stars, and More! Level 3 by Joe Rhatigan

The True Story of Balto: The Bravest Dog Ever, Level 3 by Natalie Standiford

Twisters! Level 3 by Lucille Recht Penner

Ballerina Dreams: From Orphan to Dancer, Level 4 by Michaela DePrince

Escape North! The Story of Harriet Tubman, Level 4 by Monica Culling

First Kids, Level 4 by Gibbs Davis

Helen Keller: Courage in the Dark, Level 4 by Johanna Hurwitz

Malala: A Hero for All, Level 4 by Shana Corey

Pompeii . . . Buried Alive! Level 4 by Edith Kunhardt

Spooky & Spookier: Four American Ghost Stories, Level 4 by Lori Haskins

The Great Houdini: World Famous Magician and Escape Artist, Level 4 by Monica Kulling

The Titanic: Lost and Found, Level 4 by Judy Connelly

Volcanoes: Mountains of Fire, Level 4 by Eric Arnold

Dinosaur Hunters, Level 5 by Kate McMullan

Moonwalk, Level 5 by Judy Donnelly

Raptor Pack, Level 5 by Dr. Robert T. Bakker

The Trojan Horse: How the Greeks Won the War, Level 5 by Emily Little

To the Top! Climbing the World's Highest Mountain, Level 5 by Sydelle Kramer

Trail of Tears, Level 5 by Joseph Bruchac

BOOKS FOR INDEPENDENT READING

Popular Graphic Novel Series

Amulet series by Kazu Kibuishi

Bone series by Jeff Smith

Baby Mouse series by Jennifer L. Holm and Matthew Holm

Dog Man series by Dav Pilkey

Lunch Lady series by Jarrett J. Krosoczka

The Olympians series by George O'Conner

Stargazing series by Jen Wang

Zita the Spacegirl series by Ben Hatke

Graphic Novels

All Summer Long by Hope Larson

Be Prepared by Vera Brosgol

The Cardboard Kingdom written and illustrated by Chad Sell

Drama by Raina Telgemeier

Ghosts by Raina Telgemeier

Mighty Jack by Ben Hatke

Positively Izzy by Terri Libenson

Roller Girl by Victoria Jamieson

Sisters by Raina Telgemeier

Smile by Raina Telgemeier

Snow White by Matt Phelan

Popular Illustrated Chapter Book Series

Big Nate by Lincoln Pierce

Diary of a Wimpy Kid by Jeff Kinney

Dork Diaries by Rachel Rene Russell

Origami Yoda by Tom Angelberger

Timmy Failure by Stephan Pastis

Popular Books

As Brave as You by Jason Reynolds

Brown Girl Dreaming by Jacqueline Woodson

Crenshaw by Katherine Applegate

Esperanza Rising by Pam Munoz Ryan

Inside Out and Back Again by Thannhha Lai

The Moon Within by Aida Salazar

Mufaro's Beautiful Daughters: An African Tale by John Steptoe

Ruby Bridges by Robert Coles

Smack Dab in the Middle of Maybe by Jo Watson Hackl

Stanford Wong Flunks Big Time by Lisa Yee

Too Many Tamales by Gary Soto

The Tree and Me by Bea Garcia, illustrated by Deborah Zemke

Poetry Books

Bookjoy Wordjoy by Pat Mora, illustrated by Raul Colon

Dare to Dream . . . Change the World by Jill Corcoran

The Dream Keeper and Other Poems by Langston Hughes

For Everyone by Jason Reynolds

Firefly July: A Year of Very Short Poems by Paul Janeczko

Hidden City: Poems of Urban Wildlife by Sarah Grace Tuttle, illustrated by Amy Schimler-Safford

Hip Hop Speaks to Children: A Celebration of Poetry with a Beat by Nikki Giovanni

Hoop Kings by Charles R. Smith

Honey, I Love and Other Love Poems by Eloise Greenfield

I Am Loved by Nikki Giovanni, illustrated by Ashley Bryan

Neighborhood Odes by Gary Soto and David Diaz

Out of Wonder by Kwame Alexander

A Pocketful of Poems by Nikki Grimes

The Poetry of Us: More Than 200 Poems That Celebrate the People, Places, and Passions of the United States

Poetry 180 collected by Billy Collins

Poetry for Young People: Emily Dickinson

Poetry for Young People: Langston Hughes

Poetry for Young People: Maya Angelou, editor, Dr. Edwin Graves Wilson

The Random House Book of Poetry

This Same Sky: A Collection of Poems from Around the World, selected by Naomi Shihab Nye

Middle Grade Poetry Novels

Booked by Kwame Alexander

Brown Girl Dreaming by Jacqueline Woodson

The Crossover by Kwame Alexander

Garvey's Choice by Nikki Grimes

Enchanted Air: Two Cultures, Two Wings by Margarita Engle

House Arrest by K. A. Holt

Inside Out and Back Again by Thanhha Lai

Josephine: The Dazzling Life of Josephine Baker by Patricia Huby Powell

Long Way Down by Jason Reynolds

Love That Dog by Sharon Creech

One Last Word: Wisdom from the Harlem Renaissance by Nikki Grimes

Out of the Dust by Karen Hesse

Tropical Secrets: Holocaust Refugees in Cuba by Margarita Engle

Unbound by Ann E. Burg

Up From the Sea by Leza Lowitz

You Can Fly: The Tuskegee Airmen by Carol Boston Weatherford

APPENDIX K

Picture Books for Interactive Read-Alouds

FICTION

Alma and How She Got Her Name by Juana Martinez-Neal

Carmela: Full of Wishes by Matt De La Pena, illustrated by Christian Robinson

The Day You Begin by Jacqueline Woodson, illustrated by Rafael Lopez

The Day the War Came by Nicola Davies, illustrated by Rebecca Cobb

Each Kindness by Jacqueline Woodson, illustrated by E. B. Lewis

Rescue and Jessica: A Life-Changing Friendship by Hesica Kensky and Patrick Downes, illustrated by Scott Magoon

This Is the Rope: A Story From the Great Migration by Jacqueline Woodson, illustrated by James Ransome

The Uncorker of Ocean Bottles by Michael Cuevas, illustrated by Erin E. Stead

NONFICTION

Between the Lines: How Ernie Barnes Went from the Football Field to the Art Gallery by Sandra Neil Wallace, illustrated by Bryan Collier

The First Step: How One Girl Put Segregation on Trial by Susan E. Goodman, illustrated by E. B. Lewis

Free as a Bird: The Story of Malala, written and illustrated by Lina Maslo

Hidden Figures: The True Story of Four Black Women and the Space Race by Margot Lee Shetterly, illustrated by Laura Freeman

Out of This World: The Surreal Art of Leonora Carrington by Michelle Markel, illustrated by Amanda Hall

REFERENCES

Allington, R. L. (1977). If they don't read much, how are they ever gonna get good? *Journal of Adult and Adolescent Literacy, 21*(1), 57–61.

Allington, R. L. (2002). What I've learned about effective reading instruction. *Phi Delta Kappan, 83*(10), 740–747.

Allington, R. L. (2014). How reading volume affects both reading fluency and reading achievement. *International Electronic Journal of Elementary Education, 7*(1), 13–26.

Allington, R. L., & Johnston, P.H. (2002). *Reading to learn. Lessons from exemplary classrooms.* New York, NY: Guilford.

Allington, D. (2012). *What really matters for struggling readers: Designing research-based programs.* Boston, MA: Pearson.

Anderson, R. C., Wilson P. T., & Fielding, L. G. (1988). Growth in reading and how children spend their time outside of school. *Reading Research Quarterly, 3*(23), 285–303.

Barone, D. M., & Taylor, J. (2006). *Improving students' writing, K–8: Meaning making to high stakes!* Thousand Oaks, CA: Corwin.

Beck, I. L., McKeown, M. G., & Kucan, L. (2013). *Bringing words to life: Robust vocabulary instruction.* New York, NY: Guilford.

Blachowicz, C. L. Z., & Fisher, P. J. L. (2006). *Teaching vocabulary in all classrooms.* Upper Saddle River, NJ: Pearson Education.

Brozo, W. G., Shiel, G., & Topping, K. (2008). Engage in reading: Lessons learned from three PISA countries. *Journal of Adolescent and Adult Literacy, 51*(4), 304–315.

Bryan, T. (2018). *The art of comprehension: Exploring visual texts to foster comprehension, conversation, and confidence.* Portland, ME: Stenhouse.

Burkins, J., & Yaris, K. (2018). *Who's doing the work? How to say less so readers can do more.* Portland, ME: Stenhouse.

Donahoo, J. (2016). *Collective efficacy: How educators' beliefs impact student learning.* Thousand Oaks, CA: Corwin.

De Koning, B. B., & van der Schoot, M. (2013). Becoming part of the story! Refueling the interest in visualization strategies for reading comprehension. *Educational Psychology Review, 25*(2): 261–287.

Dweck, C. S. (2007). *Mindset: The new psychology of success.* New York, NY: Random House.

Fisher, D. U., & Frey, N. (2013). *Better learning through structured teaching: A framework for the gradual release of responsibility* (2nd ed.). Alexandria, VA: ASCD.

Gambrell, L. B., Marinak, B. A. Brooker, H. R., & McCrea-Andrews. H. J. (2011). The importance of independent reading. In S. J. Samuels & A. E. Farstrup (Eds.), *What research has to say about reading instruction* (pp. 143–157). Newark, DE: International Reading Association.

Garas-York, K., & Almasi, J. F. (2017). Constructing meaning through discussion. In S. E. Israel (Ed.), *Handbook of research on reading comprehension* (2nd ed.)(pp. 500–518). New York, NY: Guildford Press.

Graham, S., Harris, K. R., & Santangelo, T. (2015). Research-based writing practices and the Common Core: Meta-analysis and meta-synthesis. *Elementary School Journal, 115*, 498–522.

Krashen, S. (2004). *The power of reading: Insights from research* (2nd ed.). Westport, CT: Libraries Unlimited.

Lian, L. A., & Galda, L. (2010). Responding and comprehending: Reading with delight and understanding. *The Reading Teacher, 63*(4), 330–333.

Meacham, M. (2017). *TMI! Cognitive overload and learning.* Retrieved from https://www.learningtogo.info/2017/02/tmi-cognitive-overload-and-learning/

Miller, D., & Sharp, C. (2018). *Game changer! Book access for all kids.* New York, NY: Scholastic.

Murray, D. M. (1984). *Write to learn.* New York, NY: Holt, Rinehart & Winston.

NAEP (National Association of Educational Assessment. (2011). National Assessment Governing Board, U.S. Department of Education.

Owacki, G., & Goodman, Y. (2002). *Kidwatching: Documenting children's literacy development.* Portsmouth, NH: Heinemann.

Pearson, P. D., & Gallagher, M. C. (1983). The instruction of reading comprehension.

Contemporary Educational Psychology, 8(3), 317–344.

Rasinski, T. (2010). *The fluent reader* (2nd ed.). New York, NY: Scholastic.

Rasinski, T., & Griffith, L. (2011). *Fluency through practice & performance.* Huntington Beach, CA: Shell Education.

Robb, L. (2017). *Read talk write: 35 lessons that teach students to analyze fiction and nonfiction.* Thousand Oaks, CA: Corwin.

Robb, L. (2014). *Vocabulary is comprehension: Getting to the root of text comprehension.* Thousand Oaks, CA: Corwin.

Rosenblatt, L. (1978). *The reader, the text, the poem: The transactional theory of the literary work.* Carbondale: Southern Illinois University Press.

Samuels, S. J., & Wu, Y.-C. (2004). *How the amount of time spent on independent reading affects reading achievement: A response to the National Reading Panel.* Retrieved from http://citeseerx.ist.psu.edu/viewdoc/summary?doi=10.1.1.539.9906

Self, J. (1987). *Plain talk about learning and writing across the curriculum.* Urbana, IL: National Council of Teachers of English.

Vygotsky, L. S. (1978). *Mind in society: The development of higher psychological processes.* Cambridge, MA: Harvard University Press.

Children's Literature Cited

Dillon, D. (2018). *I can be anything! Don't tell me I can't.* New York, NY: Blue Sky Press, Scholastic.

Goodman, S. E. (2016). *The first step: How one girl put segregation on trial.* New York, NY: Bloomsbury USA Childrens.

Jerdine, N. (2007). *Pitching in for Eubie*, New York, NY: Amistad.

Maslo, L. (2018). *Free as a bird: The story of Malala.* New York, NY: HarperCollins.

Medina, T. (2006). *Love to Langston.* New York, NY: Lee & Low Books.

Sleator, W. (1989). The elevator. In J. Yolen & M. H. Greenberg (Eds.), *Things that go bump in the night* (pp. 6–14). New York, NY: Harper & Row.

INDEX

Because...
ALL TEACHERS ARE LEADERS

LAURA ROBB

In *Read, Talk, Write*, Laura Robb lays out the classroom structures that create the time and space for students to have productive talk and written discourse about texts.

LAURA ROBB

Laura Robb provides a systematic vocabulary plan that takes just 10 to 15 minutes, much of it spent in partner and independent work. All materials are included.

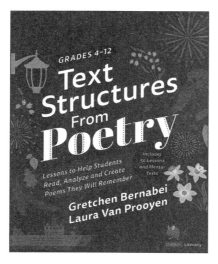

GRETCHEN BERNABEI, LAURA VAN PROOYEN

Teach your students to learn about poetry using the magic of poems themselves, and lead the way to a rewarding love of poetry for teachers and students alike.

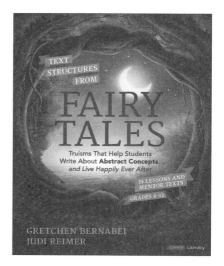

GRETCHEN BERNABEI, JUDI REIMER

Centered on classic fairy tales, 35 lessons include a writing prompt and a planning framework that leads students to organize writing through a text structure.

To order your copies, visit corwin.com/literacy

At Corwin Literacy we have put together a collection of just-in-time, classroom-tested, practical resources from trusted experts that allow you to quickly find the information you need when you need it.

DOUGLAS FISHER, NANCY FREY, NANCY AKHAVAN

Evidence-based approaches ensure that teachers have all they need to achieve balance in their literacy classrooms across a wide range of critical skills.

MATTHEW JOHNSON

Matthew Johnson offers classroom-tested solutions that not only alleviate the feedback-burnout cycle, but also lead to significant growth for students.

M. COLLEEN CRUZ

Backed by long-term academic and field research, *Writers Read Better: Narrative* presents more than 50 interconnected lesson pairs that can be implemented either as a complete curriculum or as a supplement to an existing program.

M. COLLEEN CRUZ

Complete with practical suggestions on adapting over 50 lessons to suit the particular needs of your classroom and students, *Writers Read Better: Nonfiction* offers a solid foundation for giving your students the advantage of powerful, transferable literacy skills.

A SAGE Publishing Company